Praise for

Good Mourning

"Meyer's post-college stint at a Manhattan funeral parlor yielded a memoir that's both funny and touching."

—*People*

"[A] fast, funny memoir. . . . *Good Mourning* makes perfect, macabre reading."

—*New York Post*

"A behind-the-scenes look into one of the most legendary funeral homes in the country."

—*Cosmopolitan*

"If Carrie Bradshaw worked in a funeral home à la *Six Feet Under*, her story would look something like Meyer's charming memoir about her tenure planning funerals."

—*Publishers Weekly* (starred review)

"A sweet, touching, and funny read. Meyer is truly likable, a great storyteller. . . . A lighthearted, moving glimpse into the almost beyond."

—*Booklist*

"Still grieving her dad's death, Meyer got a job at a famed NYC funeral home (of all places). Oddly enough, as she charmingly reveals, it helped her heal."

—*Good Housekeeping*

"A page-turning memoir about what goes on behind the scenes at the funeral home where anyone who's anyone in New York goes to be embalmed."

—*Town & Country*

"Meyer's new memoir, *Good Mourning*, is a hilarious and often poignant look at her time at Crawford and her life in the aftermath of her father's death."

—*Bustle*

"A lighthearted and poignant account of a job we've always found morbidly fascinating. It's also a reminder: Sometimes the silliest send-offs are the most fitting . . . and the ones that truly help us heal."

—*PureWow*

Good Mourning

Elizabeth Meyer

with Caitlin Moscatello

G
GALLERY BOOKS
New York   London   Toronto   Sydney   New Delhi

G

Gallery Books
An Imprint of Simon & Schuster, Inc.
1230 Avenue of the Americas
New York, NY 10020

First Gallery Books trade paperback edition June 2016

GALLERY BOOKS and colophon are registered trademarks
of Simon & Schuster, Inc.

For information about special discounts for bulk purchases,
please contact Simon & Schuster Special Sales at 1-866-506-1949
or business@simonandschuster.com.

The Simon & Schuster Speakers Bureau can bring authors to your
live event. For more information or to book an event, contact the
Simon & Schuster Speakers Bureau at 1-866-248-3049 or visit
our website at www.simonspeakers.com.

Interior design by Davina Mock-Maniscalco

Manufactured in the United States of America

10   9   8   7   6   5   4   3   2   1

The Library of Congress has cataloged the hardcover edition as follows:

Meyer, Elizabeth, 1985–
    Good mourning / by Elizabeth Meyer ; with Caitlin Moscatello.—First
Gallery Books hardcover edition.
        pages cm
        1. Meyer, Elizabeth, 1985– 2. Undertakers and undertaking—United
States—Biography. 3. Fathers and daughters—Biography. 4. Socialites—
United States—Biography. 5. Bereavement—Psychological aspects.
I. Moscatello, Caitlin. II. Title.
    RA622.7.M49A3 2015
    363.7'5092—dc23
    [B]
                                        2014039353

ISBN 978-1-4767-8361-1
ISBN 978-1-4767-8364-2 (pbk)
ISBN 978-1-4767-8365-9 (ebook)

To Dad, Mom, and Damon

Happiness is beneficial for the body,
but it is grief that develops the powers of the mind.
—MARCEL PROUST

Prologue

*W*e're all going to die. I'm not trying to bum you out. And I also know that somewhere, deep down, you are perfectly aware of the fact that none of us will be here forever. Death is a tough topic—it's scary to think about dying, and it's not any *less* scary to think about losing someone you love. So we have a tendency to not talk about "the end" and all the things that come with it: funerals, gravestones, the nail-biting decision of whether to adorn your loved one's casket with orchids or peonies.

But not you, who picked up this book and thought, *Give me some of that sweet funeral knowledge!* You're not afraid. You're open-minded. And I dig that about you.

Not everyone is so relaxed when it comes to death, though. In fact, sometimes the people who have it all in this life are the ones who are most afraid of it. I guess when everything around you is so gosh-darn fabulous, you don't want the curtains to close. I get that. But even the people in the high-society circle I've been running in since I was born can't escape the same fate as . . . well . . . every living thing ever. (I know, I know . . . *Did she really just say "high society"?* But there's just no term for the people I grew up around that doesn't solicit an eye roll. Trust me. I've Googled.) I guess what I'm trying to say is, death is hard for a lot of us to accept . . . and perhaps especially difficult for people who are accustomed to getting what they want, when they want it. "Yes, your car is waiting for you." "Yes, we'll find you a table." "Yes, we can custom-make that for you." "No" is simply not part of their vocabulary. "No, there is not a cure." "No, there isn't anything else we can do." "No, it won't make a difference if you pay me in Louis Vuitton suitcases filled with cash."

Don't get me wrong, the purpose of this book isn't to make fun of a bunch of silly rich people; in fact, I changed names and identifying details. If anything, death is the one experience other than birth that unifies all of us—from the guy who drives the limo to the CEO of the company who built its engine. And since we can't avoid it, well, I figure we might as well embrace what we've got coming. That's part of the reason I got into the death business in the first place. When I was twenty-one and most of my friends were *Daddy-do-you-know-someone?*-ing their way into fancy banks and

PR firms, I was grieving the loss of my father, who had just died of cancer. That's how I found myself in the lobby of Crawford Funeral Home, one of several premier funeral homes in Manhattan, begging for a job one day. This might not be politically correct, but I'm just going to say it: anyone who's anyone in New York City—or rather, anyone who's anyone who's *dead* in New York City—winds up at Crawford. It's where loved ones said good-bye to everyone from John Lennon and Jackie O to Heath Ledger and Philip Seymour Hoffman. If you can afford it, it's just *where you go.* One last social gathering to finish off a lifetime of champagne toasts.

Of course, not everyone in my life thought that my sudden desire to hang around dead people was as amazing as I did. Seriously, you would have thought I'd traded in all my Armani gowns for some goth-chick combat boots and black lipstick. My best friend, Gaby, thought I was having a quarter-life crisis. My mom, well, she had to practically hold herself up against her Nancy Corzine sofa when I told her the news. "But, Elizabeth," she said, her perfectly manicured nails digging into the velvet. "You could work in *fashion.*" Even my brother, Max, who usually doesn't give a damn what I do as long as it doesn't embarrass him (for which I should probably apologize now), was concerned. "Does this have to do with Dad?" he asked late one night when he called from his prestigious white-shoe law firm. "Mom's worried."

Maybe it *was* a little weird for a woman in her early twenties to choose to work at a funeral home—and I'm sure my dad's death had *something* to do with it. But mainly, I think I liked being there for people when they needed it the most. I've said it a million times: just because you pull up to a funeral in a Bentley wearing Dior doesn't mean that it hurts any less. Death is death. Grief is grief. And as it turns out, I have a gift for planning last hurrahs for the richest of the rich (and sometimes the craziest of the crazy) so that their families can feel comfort during a really difficult time. When clients walked into the foyer of Crawford, with its ginormous ceilings and eight-foot oil paintings, I would greet them and they'd instantly relax. As one old lady in pearls once told me: "I can tell you're one of *us.*"

But things didn't always run so smoothly. There was the time I lost a body, the time I had to deal with a dead man's two wives (not ex-wives, *wives*), the time I urgently raced around Crawford looking for a fucking brain. In my years there, well, I saw it all. And like any good funeral planner, I've kept those stories locked up tight.

Until now.

ONE

It Starts with an Ending

*Y*ou know that feeling when someone tells you bad news, and for a second, it's like you're watching someone else's life happen to *your* life? And then, after you've had a moment to absorb it all, there's this moment of panic. You realize you can't fast-forward to the happy scene where all the characters break out in a dance or clink their glasses of wine together over a table because *Whew, thank God that's over. Now somebody roll the freaking credits.* That's how I felt when my dad, whom the rest of the world knew as Brett Meyer, told me he had cancer. If my life had a soundtrack, the music would have stopped in that moment. *My dad? Cancer? Impossible.*

That's not my movie—at least, I was naïve enough to think it wasn't when I was sixteen. Up until then, my life had been about ski vacations to Vail, weekend trips to Palm

Beach, and partying with my best friend, Gaby. Know where we had our Sweet Sixteen? At a club in New York's hip Meatpacking District. It was total excess: bamboo invitations to three hundred friends, Mark Ronson at the turntables, a gaggle of models circling around the dance floor. Gaby and I spent half the night sneaking Long Island Iced Teas and cosmopolitans into the bathroom (those seemed cool to drink at the time) and the other half grinding up against prep-school boys trying to move their Ferragamo loafers to a beat. At that point, the biggest problem in my life was whether we should go with buttercream or fondant for our five-tier birthday cake.

To his credit, my dad didn't want to make a big deal about the whole cancer thing, and so after the initial shock of his diagnosis, my mom, Francesca; my brother, Max; and I went back to business as usual. Dad occasionally scooted to the hospital for a quick chemo treatment, but we treated it more like he was going to a hair appointment—a weekly "touch-up" to make sure no roots were peeking through. He never acted like he was going to die, or like death was even a possibility, and so we didn't think that way, either. Even nine years later, my mom can hardly believe that he's gone. "I never once thought this would happen," she says. Mom has always been a realist but still thought, as most of us do, that the bad stuff—the cancer, the car accident, the overdose— happened to other people. Not her. Not her family. Not my dad.

Part of what made Dad seem so untouchable was his personality—you just couldn't shake him. One of my favorite stories is from early in my parents' marriage when they took a trip to Key Biscayne, Florida. Dad got this idea to rent a catamaran, even though my mom thought they should play it safe on the beach. (This was a common theme in their marriage: Dad was the adventurer, Mom was the voice of reason . . . or at least practicality.) "Something *always* goes wrong," she said to him. But Dad was all, "No, no, it'll be great!" and—thanks to his lawyer skills and a smile that always got her—they went. A couple of hours later, there they were on the catamaran, watching the sunset, when the thing *split in half.* Mom wasn't a great swimmer, so she hung on to a piece of the broken boat, bobbing up and down in the water, as the sky grew darker and darker. "Are there sharks?" she asked my dad, terrified. He looked around, treading water. "Probably," he said, as if he were talking about guppies. A couple of hours later—yes, *hours*—a boat finally noticed them and came to the rescue. Know what Dad wanted to do the next day? Go sailing.

Mom settled into the Upper East Side well, but she grew up in a working-class neighborhood in Queens—the type of place where big Italian families got together after church every week for macaroni and Sunday sauce. While Dad studied at an expensive private university in New England, she was keeping it real living at home while going to college in the city. In fact, they probably wouldn't have met—Lord knows their social circles never overlapped—if my mom hadn't randomly befriended an acquaintance of my father's while she was on vacation. By the time her plane landed back in New York, she already had a missed call from my dad. She only called him back because *her* mom insisted it was rude not to at least respond, and she eventually agreed to go out with him for the sole reason that he asked her out for a Tuesday. Mom had other options, and she was not keen on giving up a Saturday night for some what's-his-face on the other side of the river.

Dad, on the other hand, grew up in a mansion in Scarsdale—an affluent New York suburb where extravagant homes line the streets and people have pool houses and gardeners. His mom, Elaine, was less than welcoming when Dad brought home a girl from Queens. My mom still talks about the horror of their first dinner: Elaine kept kicking under the table, shouting, "It's not working! It's not working!" Only later did Mom realize that the "it" was a bell attached to a wire used to signal the help, either to clear a plate or fetch her something from the kitchen because *God forbid she get up*. Dad, who had cut the wire, laughed off his crazy mother's behavior—something he was always able to do. (Me? Not as much. Elaine—yes, I called my grandmother by her first name—was the epitome of a society snob.) Even at stuffy charity dinners and black-tie parties, Dad was always able to keep a sense of humor about the whole thing—the money, the people, the *scene*. He used to

say, "Never own something you can't afford to lose, Lizzie."
I never forgot it.

So when it became clear that, after he'd been fighting
cancer for five years, I might actually lose my dad—the one
thing I couldn't imagine living without—I struggled to wrap
my head around it. I started to treat Dad's hospital stay like
he was shacking up at a nearby hotel. After a night clubbing
with friends from New York University (where I went to college so that I could stay close to my father), I'd head to a
bagel shop at five a.m., pick up a half dozen soft, doughy
pieces of heaven and a tub of cream cheese to share with the
nurses, and head to Dad's hospital room for breakfast. He
never said a word about my probably too-short skirts or
probably too-high heels. We'd just talk about how the Giants
played last weekend and if they had a shot in hell on Sunday.

Then one morning before a major surgery—one that he
might not make it out of, the doctors told us—my father finally admitted that there was a chance, a slight chance, that
he wasn't going to be there to do all the things we'd planned.
There might not be another trip up to our country house in
the Berkshires, where Dad used to pull my friends and me
on an inflatable tube around a frozen lake from the back of a
four-wheeler. There might not be another family trip to Europe, or sail up the Hudson, or even early-morning bagel
breakfast; no more father-daughter dates to the Met Ball or
summertime canoe races. There might not be more of our
favorite things, because time might be up.

And then, just like that, it was.

I remember getting the call: I was out walking our black Lab, Maggie, and didn't have my phone on me, but I just got this feeling in the pit of my stomach—something told me to get home, and fast. When I ran through the door, I grabbed my cell phone without so much as taking off my coat and saw that I had ten missed calls from Max and my mom. I didn't check the messages. I didn't have to. I knew what this meant. The only person I did reach out to was Elaine. I knew she was on her way to the airport, eager to get back to her bridge games and Russian wolfhounds, affectionately and ridiculously named Smirnoff One and Smirnoff Two. (For all her fantastic taste in designer clothes and vintage cars, Elaine had terrible taste in booze.) I figured she'd want to have the car swing back around ASAP to the hospital— this was her son, after all. But instead she just sighed into the phone. "Lovey girl, I *have* to get back." Elaine had never been maternal—I'd never once seen her even hug my dad, and the only way she ever showed me affection (if you can call it that) was by tapping on her nose and demanding a kiss. *On her nose.* Although, what can you expect from a woman who hid a bell under the table to summon her staff?

When I returned to the hospital, Dad was lying in his bed, with Max standing behind him and my mom at his side. My uncle—Dad's brother—was also there with his wife. The doctors explained what was about to happen: Dad needed to be put into an induced coma so that they could try to elevate his white blood cell count. First, they would need to stick a tube down this throat. After that, he would be on a ventilator and would soon be completely unresponsive. They were clear that the odds were stacked against us, and there was a good chance Dad might not wake up—ever. But they were also clear that there was no other option except to take no chances—very unlike Dad—and lose him anyway within days, even hours.

I walked around to the other side of the bed, opposite from where my mom was standing, and held my dad's other hand. He looked up at me calmly, even though he knew exactly what was going on. "I love you," I said, somehow managing to stick to the group's code of not crying, not even now. "It'll be fine," Dad replied.

I stroked his hand while a nurse pushed the breathing tube down his throat and then as they wheeled him away. For the next two days, Max and I swapped turns sitting by Dad's side in the ICU. Max read him short stories by Kurt Vonnegut, and I talked to him about nothing in particular— although I did ask him, *beg him*, a few times not to leave me. "What would I do without you?" I asked, sometimes jokingly, other times desperately. I wondered if it was true what they say about people in comas being able to hear and feel you. Staring at my father lying there, hooked up to a gazillion machines, it was hard to imagine that was possible. In a lot of ways, I wished that he had already gone somewhere else. If he'd been able to speak, I'm sure he would have said something like, "This place sucks. I mean, talk about a bunch of stiffs. Let's get out of here."

Finally the doctors told us what we already knew—Dad wasn't coming out of it. So we once again gathered around his bed, my mom and I each taking one of his hands, and prepared ourselves for another good-bye . . . this time, the final one. The machine with Dad's vitals went from *beep-beep-beep* to *beep . . . beep . . .* to one long, steady beep, just the way you think it does. And while my heart was aching, the scene itself lacked much drama.

Before we headed out to the garage to get the car, I grabbed Dad's cell phone—which was still ringing with calls from clients and friends, many of whom he had never even told he was sick. Up until his death, Dad had still been holding meetings in his hospital room, where a bunch of associates from his office (they of course knew he was sick, but not *that* sick) would stand around and debrief him on this case or that case, while Dad told them how to handle things. He had never let on that he might not make it—and so there it was, a cell phone filled with missed calls and voice mails, going off once again.

"Hello, this is Elizabeth speaking," I answered, trying to keep my voice steady even though my mind was spinning. *Is this really happening?* I thought. *Am I really answering Dad's phone, because Dad is gone?*

"Hi there, Elizabeth. Can you put Brett on? We have a question and I think he—"

"I'm so sorry, but my father isn't available."

"Oh. Okay. Well, just tell him tha—"

"He passed away," I said, blurting the words out, getting them over with.

"What?"

I took a deep breath, willing myself to say it again. The room spun faster. "He passed away. It just happened."

Silence.

More silence.

"Oh my God."

"We'll be in touch with the firm as soon as we've made arrangements," I said, a weird numbness setting in.

There was another missed call—several, actually—from Elaine. She'd been dialing me, Max, and Mom, one after the other, for the past few hours, and we'd all been hitting "ignore." I listened to her voice mail, which said, and I kid you not: "Lovey girl. It's Nanny calling. I've started running a bath. I'd like to know how your father is before I get in. And you know nobody likes to soak in cold water. Call me."

I felt a wave of rage come over me. She knew damn well when she strapped her tweed-covered ass into her first-class seat on the plane that she was never going to see her son again. *How is he doing?? Are you fucking kidding me??* I picked up the phone, dialed her number, and barely let her voice ring in my ear before opening my mouth:

"He's dead," I said. Then I hung up.

When I got back to my parents' Fifth Avenue apartment,

it occurred to me that everything should be different—and yet everything was the same. Maggie wiggled to greet us at the door, unaware of what we'd all just lost. A copy of the *New York Times* from that morning remained on the entrance table, unread. The silver picture frames on the living room mantel tilted just so—each filled with images of my father and my whole family in happier times, staring back at me as if to ask, *Why so sad, Lizzie?*

I grabbed my phone, wrapped myself in a yellow cashmere blanket, and slumped onto the edge of the couch. Then I looked up the number for Crawford Funeral Home, just a couple of blocks away, to schedule an appointment. It might sound weird that at twenty-one, I was the one who took on the responsibility of arranging my father's funeral. But to be honest, I didn't trust anyone else to get it right. Besides, unlike my mom and brother, who were being comforted by adoring friends and family in the next room and noshing on some of the pounds and *pounds* of catered food our family had ordered (Italians grieve with carbs), I preferred to be alone. A few minutes later, I had an appointment scheduled with the funeral director for the next morning.

I didn't sleep. I'm not sure anybody did. For one thing, our apartment was buzzing with people well past midnight—I couldn't tell if they were grieving and wanted to connect to Dad, through us, or if they felt bad and didn't want to leave Mom, Max, and me alone. Normally, I would be the one walking around filling people's drinks and turning up the music, but I couldn't will myself off that couch. I had even hoisted poor Maggie onto it with me, using her as a pillow. It wasn't until Gaby—fresh off a plane from Los Angeles—rushed through the door and threw her arms around me that I finally felt a sense of calm. While most people wouldn't put their thousand-dollar vicuña shawl anywhere near someone's teary, snot-covered face, she pulled me in as close to her as I could get. Gaby was the one person who didn't ask me if I was okay. She knew I wasn't. She wasn't really, either. We both loved my dad.

At seven a.m., I took Maggie out to Central Park, her absolute favorite time to go for a walk since dogs are allowed to roam off-leash early in the morning. Afterward, I took off my clothes—the same ones I had been wearing for more than twenty-four hours—and dragged myself into the shower. I let the hot water run over me and again fell into a deep cry, this time with no one to comfort me. Dad was gone. He wasn't on a business trip. He wasn't at the hospital. Yesterday, with its quiet beginning and hectic ending, was not a dream. A heavy weight built up in my chest until I let out a deep sob—the kind of cry that starts way down inside of you and comes out like a gasp of air. My tears mixed with the water pouring down from the showerhead, and for twenty minutes, I sat on the floor, too exhausted to hold myself up. After I physically couldn't cry anymore, I took a deep breath, toweled myself off, and looked in the mirror. "Okay, Lizzie, get it together," I said to myself, channeling as much of my father's strength as I could.

"ELIZABETH, WELCOME. We're so sorry for your loss," said a woman in a black suit standing in the Crawford foyer. I felt like I had walked right into a mausoleum—the outside of the building was smooth brown stone, and the inside, at least upon entering, wasn't much more inviting. "Tony, our funeral director, will be with you in a moment."

She left me standing on the ornate green rug, staring up at the absolutely huge chandelier that hung from the twenty-foot ceiling like a spider from a web. I was immediately overwhelmed with the smell of lilies. If you've ever been to a wake, you know why: florists love to put lilies in floral arrangements for funerals. It's like the unofficial death flower. I decided then that I would not let lilies invade Dad's service.

My first impression of Tony was that he looked like Tony Soprano—just with gelled-back, prematurely gray hair. He was smartly dressed in a black suit and red tie, although the poor stitching and slightly shiny fabric were a dead giveaway that he was *not* in designer duds. But, he had the right smile for the occasion: friendly, but not happy. I mean, any time someone walked through Crawford's door, it was because they were experiencing one of the worst moments in their lives. He couldn't exactly greet them with a wide grin and a kiss on both cheeks.

Tony led me to his office, which looked like it hadn't been updated in decades. All the furniture was a dark wood, and the drapes, the rugs, the oil paintings—they all just looked so . . . *heavy*. It was kind of how I felt; even though I'd lost ten pounds in the past month, I was weighed down with grief. "We've got floral arrangements you can choose from, and I'll take you to the casket room," he said, pushing a book with photos of—you guessed it—lilies across the desk. I shuddered a little looking at a giant baseball made of white carnations and red roses and pushed the book back across the table.

"No," I said. "But thank you."

"No? I mean, we have other options, we can do whatever you—"

"I have my own plans for Dad's funeral, and what I want is for this not to feel like a funeral at all. For starters, I don't want any flowers like this. I want peonies." (Peonies are my mom's favorite flower, and while I knew Dad wouldn't care about the blooms, I was sure he'd be happy for her to have that little piece of comfort.)

"Peonies are out of season," said Tony, shaking his head. "Most people couldn't get them for you, but I can. They'll have to be flown in from Brazil. It will be expensive, but it will be great."

"That's fine," I said. "Just get white peonies."

Tony sat up straighter in his chair.

Our next stop was the casket room. Dad was going to be cremated, but thanks to my pricey floral selection, Tony was onto my affinity for luxury. Rather than just suggest a standard poplar-wood casket, Tony led me toward a white casket lined in powder-blue velvet, a mahogany casket with pops of gold on the handles, and the pièce de résistance, a casket made entirely from bronze. "This is a beauty," he said, running his hands along the edges. "Of course, it's metal, so it can't be used for a cremation."

"How much?" I asked.

"This one is ninety thousand."

"Dollars?"

Even in my grief, or maybe *especially* because I was grieving, I was annoyed that Tony would even show me such a ridiculously priced casket. What kind of insane person would spend that much money on a box, especially for someone who wasn't even going to be buried in it?

I spent hours walking Tony through my vision for Dad's funeral. There would be no boring hymns. No tragic eulogies. If there was one thing I knew for certain, it was that Dad would want us to celebrate his life with a party, not some sob fest. And if there was anyone who could give him that, it was me. I'd spent years planning events for friends. Granted, they were usually to celebrate a grand opening or a significant birthday, but this wouldn't be that different. Trade out a hip-hop DJ for a jazz ensemble, centerpieces for a casket spray, and invitations for prayer cards, and boom, the perfect send-off.

The night before the service, I called Gaby and asked her to pick out a black dress for me. She came over with two Fendi sheath dresses—one for me, and one for her. "It's the same dress," I said, stating the obvious. It was so Gaby to do something like that. Everyone always assumed when they met her that, since she was the daughter of a famous rock star, she would be some ditzy, spoiled brat, but that couldn't be further from the truth. She had a huge heart—and great taste. I gave her a hug, thankful for her sign of solidarity.

I wanted to get to Crawford right when it opened at eight a.m. to make sure that Tony had set everything up exactly as I had asked, so I jumped out of bed even before my alarm went off at seven and slipped into the Fendi dress and a pair of Jimmy Choos. I looked out the window onto the mostly empty sidewalks, the rest of the Upper East Side still sipping their lattes or under their pressed Egyptian-cotton sheets. For them, this would be just another day. I turned from the window and clasped on my dad's Rolex. He hadn't officially left it to me, but there was an unspoken understanding that I would be the one to wear it. There had always been alliances in our house: Mom and Max were a team, feeding off of each other's practicality and general anxiety, and then there was me and Dad, always up to something fabulous and fun. While I love my mother—she's one of the strongest people I've ever met—Dad was my person. I always knew he had my back. Even my mom seemed to recognize that Dad's death would affect me in a different way than my brother. She certainly wasn't going to say anything when I grabbed his watch. Nobody was.

"Are you ready?" Mom asked from the hallway. Turns out, she and Max hadn't gotten much sleep either. Since we were all ready to go, we decided to walk over to Crawford together.

Tony was the first person to greet us. He paid special attention to my mother, carefully directing her into the room where my father's casket was displayed, along with framed photos of him from different points of his life. There it was: Dad on a sailboat, Dad with his best friend, Dad piling sand onto the yard at our country house to create a "beach." A whole life laid out in still images, which I had delivered in a box the day before. Mom saw the white peonies and put her hands over her mouth. "Oh," she said, holding her hand to her chest, her eyes filling with tears.

"Where's the restroom?" I asked, needing a minute to myself. Tony directed me down the hall. Just as I turned the corner toward the ladies' room, I bumped into another man in a black suit holding a large makeup bag.

"You have more makeup than I do," I said, smiling.

The man smiled back softly. "Sorry," he said. "Didn't mean to get in your way."

"It's fine," I said. "I'm Liz, Brett's daughter."

"So sorry for your loss, Elizabeth," said the man. He had

an accent similar to Tony's, but more wrinkles than him and warm blue eyes. "I'm Bill."

I thought I had heard Tony mention his name. "Are you the embalmer?" I asked.

Bill looked uncomfortable, shifting from one foot to the other. "That would be me," he said. "Again, so sorry about your dad."

What else can you say to someone who just lost their favorite person?

When I got back to the chapel, I noticed that all of the additional chairs the staff had brought in for overflow guests were going to create a traffic jam near the casket. "They all need to go to the back of the room," I said out loud, looking around to see if I could find Tony. I'd planned enough events to know that if things got really crowded, as I suspected they might, we'd need the space for standing room.

Mom shook her head. "There's no need. This service is just for family and very close friends. There will only be a small group of us," she said.

An hour later, more than five hundred people were lined up out the door of the funeral home. There were, of course, old friends and neighbors, family members and colleagues from the law firm. There were also Dad's clients—rap stars and fashion moguls, famous entertainers and their entourages. (Only in Manhattan can a funeral double as a place to see and be seen.)

I wasn't surprised by the diverse crowd. That was the thing about Dad—he made everyone feel like a close friend.

I busied myself greeting people as they entered the room. Instead of boring hymns, David Bowie and the Rolling Stones buzzed from the speakers. I hugged everyone at the door, trying to signal that this was an upbeat affair—it was okay to laugh and share stories. Once traffic was moving steadily to the front of the room, I ran over to find Max, who was nervously holding a copy of the eulogy we had written together. "You about ready?" I said. Don't get me wrong—I was nervous too. But Max and I had spent hours deciding which details of Dad's life to share with a room full of people who loved him. I had a feeling we'd bring the house down. And if not, well, what kind of terrible person is going to criticize a eulogy?

"Thank you all for coming today," I said, looking at the rows and rows of faces. So many people were crowded into the room that even those lined up against the wall were standing four rows deep. I saw my mom clutch the tissues in her hand and take a deep breath. Max and I then proceeded to tell our favorite stories about Dad. It had been hard to narrow them down, but I took special joy in telling everyone about the time Dad was asked to bring the "gifts" up to the altar at Christmas mass. Dad was Jewish—he only went to midnight mass with my mom every year because it meant a lot to her. After more than two decades of marriage, Mom decided to kick things up a notch and volunteered herself and my dad to walk the wine and Eucharist down the aisle to the priest. Dad was excited to have a special part in the ceremony—he'd been passively participating for years, sitting, then standing; standing, then kneeling; up and down, up and down. He couldn't wait to bring the gifts to the altar, because who doesn't love presents? On the night of the mass, just seconds before they walked down the aisle, Dad looked puzzled as they handed him a metal bowl with a cloth over it. "Ohhh," he said, slightly disappointed. "*These* gifts." He recovered from the disappointment that his role was not to play Santa Claus, and after he deposited the bowl of wafers with the priest, he gave a thumbs-up on his way back to the pew while the other churchgoers looked on. Many of them knew my dad and that he was Jewish and playing along for his family.

Laughter echoed through the room as Max and I took turns, growing more confident in our eulogizing abilities with each crazy story. It gave me a thrill to see people crying from laughter—those were the tears Dad would have wanted. When Max and I finished our speech, a friend of mine from high school, Jen, threw her arms around me. Like plenty of people I grew up with, Jen's parents were almost entirely absent from her life. A nanny had raised her. A chauffeur had driven her to school and ballet class. Her father, a big-time financier, stopped by our high school graduation but left before she even walked the stage to get her diploma because he "had a meeting." "It should have been my dad," she said. "It's not fair." (Before you judge her for saying something so awful, let me vouch for Jen and say her dad really was a trash can.)

I gave Jen a squeeze and told her to look around. There were wet eyes here and there, but for the most part, people were talking, hugging, even dancing. "Dad would have been proud of you," Max said as the last of the visitors filed out of the room. I waited for his typical sarcasm to follow, but it never did.

By the time I got back to the apartment, most of the people who had come to grieve my father were standing in the grand foyer, sipping Lillet and Macallan 18 and pillaging a table topped with so much food, you would have thought we were holding a charity gala. Everyone wanted to hug me. Some of the hugs were warm and comforting, others were tense and awkward. Even though the party was going strong, I was starting to feel the fatigue of the previous few days weighing down on me. I retreated to the formal living room—one of the places in the house I never typically hung out—and hoped nobody would notice.

"Lizzie, why are you crying?" asked Elaine. She had graced us all with her presence, able to leave her hectic schedule of bridge tournaments and dinners on Worth Avenue in Palm Beach. I couldn't believe it; she legitimately looked puzzled.

"I'm just tired," I said, barely able to look at her. We'd never been close, and I was always fine with that. But I'd never actually hated her until now. She was wearing an all-white pantsuit that matched her hair. You'd have thought she was going to a summer party in the Hamptons instead of, oh, I don't know . . . *her son's funeral.*

Elaine shrugged, and after telling me about all the fabulous people she got to catch up with at Dad's service, she finally left me alone. The only people I wanted near me were Gaby and my friend Ben, who had grown up in the same building as me. Ben loved my dad and was especially a fan of his blueberry pancakes. Even when we were teenagers, Ben would stop by in the morning before school just to have breakfast with Dad and me. "Mr. Meyer," he would say, plopping his backpack on one of the dining room chairs and taking a seat without having to be asked, "pass the syrup!"

When eleven o'clock came around, Gaby pulled me off the couch. "It's safe, mostly everybody has left," she said. I hadn't eaten real food in several days, and I could see Ben was already making a plate for me. A few stragglers—mostly my mom's friends who were too nervous to leave her side—came over just as I was about to attempt a bite. "Elizabeth! Oh! You did such a wonderful job," said Mrs. Mullen, a woman my mom had met at Christie's auction house. "I want you to plan my funeral! But, you know, not for a long time. Ha!" I slapped on a fake smile and nodded. It was the only reaction I had left.

Finally, the apartment was empty. Max had gone out with a group of friends—his method of grieving was to surround himself with people and talk about anything except *the* thing. The distraction technique. Mom busied herself with paperwork. She had stacks of hospital bills to deal with, but even more, she had all of Dad's investments. On her side of the family, stock portfolios looked after by private wealth managers did not exist. "How am I going to figure this out?" I heard her mutter from the other end of the dining table, her head resting on her left hand, and Dad's heavy, monogrammed silver Montblanc pen in her right. She looked so small sitting there alone at a table that sat sixteen. I should have comforted her, but I didn't. I'd always had an easy relationship with Dad, but with Mom, things were more complicated. Now she was all I had left, and even though it sounds unfair, part of me resented her for it. She had willingly dedicated her whole life to caring for my father when he needed it the most, but he was dead. It wasn't rational, but I felt that *she* had failed. *She* had let him die. She had promised things would be okay, and they weren't.

Finally alone in my bedroom, I kicked off my Jimmy Choos, unzipped my dress and let it fall to the floor, and threw on a massive sweatshirt. It felt good to wipe off the waterproof mascara and unclip my pearl necklace. I didn't have to put on a face anymore. I crawled into bed and pulled the comforter up to my chest. The room was totally dark, except for the city streetlights glowing through the curtains. There was one thing I had kept on: Dad's Rolex. I looked down at the red face and felt a wave of panic rush from my stomach to my chest and back again.

"Dad," I whispered, practically choking on the hurt. "What am I supposed to do now?" I lay there, numb, for what could have been minutes or hours. My only comfort was knowing I had thrown my father the best send-off I possibly could. Mulling that over, I somehow finally, *finally* drifted off to sleep.

When I woke up, I had the craziest idea.

TWO

Getting My Feet Wet

"Is Tony here?" I asked, looking at my watch. It was ten a.m. on a Tuesday—almost a month after Dad's funeral—and while I normally would have been just waking up from a night of dancing at Marquee (at the time, the hottest club in the city), I instead found myself standing in the foyer of Crawford, with Maggie tied up outside, finally ready to go through with my crazy plan.

The receptionist at the front desk barely raised her head to look at me. "Name?" she asked.

"Oh, he's not expecting me," I said. "I was just hoping I could talk to him. About a job."

She finally looked up and raised her eyebrows. "You wanna work here?"

I nodded. "I'm just hoping I can speak with him. I was

here last month, for my father's funeral. Brett Meyer? I'm not sure we met, though. My name's Liz."

The woman muttered something and picked up the phone. She looked like she was in her midthirties, with long dark hair and fake pink nails. She whispered something into the phone and then turned to the receptionist next to her. I had no idea what they were saying because they were speaking Spanish, but apparently it was hilarious.

"Was that Tony?" I asked. I was starting to feel self-conscious. I'd only studied French and Latin.

"What? Oh. Yeah. He's coming. You can wait over there," she said.

I awkwardly strolled around the lobby looking at a painting of Grandpa Crawford, who founded the funeral home decades earlier and ushered his son into the family business. I would later learn this was the norm. Working in death isn't something most people choose—it kind of chooses them.

"Liz, what can I do for you?" said Tony, walking up behind me.

I felt the stares of both receptionists and pulled my Hermès bag behind me. "Maybe we can talk in your office?"

I plopped myself down in the same leather chair where I had laid out the plans for Dad's funeral. "I'm wondering if you have any job openings," I said. No sense in beating around the bush.

Tony scratched his head, like he didn't quite understand.

"I have lots of experience planning events—mostly charity fund-raisers and that sort of thing for friends, although I know a lot of people in the restaurant and nightclub businesses, too. I used those skills to help plan my father's funeral, so I'm thinking . . . I could keep doing that?"

"You don't want to work here," he said, looking at his watch and letting out a sigh. "Why would a girl like you want to work at a funeral home?"

"I know your clientele," I said. "I know them better than anyone here, I bet."

Tony shuffled a stack of papers in front of him. Dead silence.

"The only opening I have is for a secretary," he said. "But you'd have to join our union, and it only pays like thirty grand a year." He shrugged. "That's it. I'm telling you, you don't want—"

"I'll take it!" I said, smiling. I wasn't sure why, but something about being back at Crawford felt right. Plus, I figured if I got bored, I could always quit and go intern or go back to event planning. (Although the latter kind of made me want to vomit; it seemed like no matter what party I was asked to plan, the next question was always, "And can you get your famous friends to come?") This was like event planning, but I didn't have to make the guest list, and the guest of honor would never be a pain in the ass.

A few minutes later, I was at the front desk filling out paperwork as quickly as possible—mostly union stuff, and copies of my photo ID. "Well, that was easy!" I said to the receptionist, who looked barely awake. "Looks like we'll be working together," I continued, convinced that she'd warm up to me, as people usually did. *She must have had a rough morning. Shame*, I thought. "Uh-huh," she said, taking the paperwork from me and tossing it in a pile next to the phone. Maggie was less than thrilled when I got back to the sidewalk, but she was easily appeased once I stopped at a nearby bakery to get her an organic dog cookie—her favorite. I bought myself a celebratory Linzer cookie as well. I hadn't expected to be offered a job on the spot, although things like that had a way of working out for me. "Maggie, isn't this exciting?" I said as we both bit into our cookies. "I'm going to plan fabulous funerals!"

I invited Max and Gaby over for dinner that night to tell them the news. Max said I would last two weeks, tops, but to my surprise, he didn't try to talk me out of it. Gaby was more worried about whether or not my job would interfere with our plans to go to London for a friend's birthday bash the following weekend. I shrugged.

"I don't have my schedule yet, but it's possible."

"Well, you could always quit, I guess."

"I haven't even started," I said, mixing a Ketel One and club soda. "Plus I'm not going to quit a job to go to a party, that's insane."

"You can't miss it! It's going to be the party *of the year*. I will seriously freak out if you don't come with."

Max pointed to my drink. "You better make that a double before you call Mom to tell her about your glamorous gig as a death secretary," he said. "Or actually, maybe spare us from the scene and just tell her in person tomorrow."

I hadn't spoken to Mom in two days, and not by accident. Max was always her favorite—she loved talking to her friends about her son, "the lawyer." He fit into her mold of what someone raised on the Upper East Side *should* be; he went to an elite grade school and the right college, got into a top law school, and chose a respectable career. Straight and narrow. I, on the other hand, had defied her from the day I could dress myself. First it was jeans instead of a smock dress, and then the stakes grew. By the time I was eighteen, I was rebelling on a higher level. I went to NYU (she pushed me to leave New York for college) and spent most of my monthly allowance on flights to Europe instead of groceries. While Dad had encouraged me to forge my own path, Mom hadn't always been impressed by my boldness. I felt deep down that she didn't trust me, that she feared my heart would lead me someplace I shouldn't go. I knew that a union job at a funeral home was *not* what she had in mind for her only daughter.

I was right.

The next night, I told Mom that I wanted to talk to her about something and that I'd be stopping by after dinner. She was tired, but in some ways, that made her seem easier to talk to. I sat down on the couch and waited for her to sit next to me, but instead she just stood behind the sofa.

"So, I have some news," I said, slightly terrified.

"Mmm-hmm," she said. "Go on."

"I . . . I got a job . . . at Crawford," I said, immediately wishing I had just told her I'd gotten a job, period.

"The funeral home?"

"Yeah. They are looking for a receptionist, and I think I could be really good at it."

Mom was silent. *Well, this is going awesome*, I thought.

"You think you could be really good at *being a receptionist*," she said, drawing out the last three words like they caused physical pain coming out of her mouth. "A lifetime of private school tuition and a two-hundred-thousand-dollar college education, and you *think* you could be a *secretary*. Is that what I'm hearing?"

The lady had a point; I probably should have considered leaving the job title out. My mom's mom, Rose, who grew up in a small apartment and never went to college, had worked as a secretary when my mom was growing up. When my parents got married, Mom worried that the money would change things—or more accurately, she worried that Max and I would become bratty little rich kids. But at the same time, over the years, I think she started to take pride in the fact that we had more opportunities than she'd grown up with. We were born into a certain lifestyle, and in Mom's opinion, the very least we could do was be grateful and take advantage of that fact.

Mom rubbed her temples and then braced herself up

against her designer sofa. I could see the frustration in her face and regretted coming over at all. "But, Elizabeth," she blurted out, "you . . . you're . . . you're pretty! And looks don't last forever, you know. They just don't. Work in PR. Work in fashion. But for goodness' sake, don't work at a *funeral home.*"

"Because what would your friends think, right?" I said, getting defensive.

"No," said Mom, shaking her head. "Because you can do better. Why would you want to be around dead people all the time? It's so, so . . . *morbid.* Is this about your father? Do you want me to call a therapist?"

I grabbed my coat, wanting to leave before losing my shit on a grieving widow. *Why can't you just be happy that I've found something I want to do?* I thought. Before Mom could say anything else, I'd walked out the front door and was charging toward the elevator. I could feel my heartbeat pounding in my ears. *She just doesn't get it.*

THE GREETING from the Spanish-speaking Crawford receptionist, Monica, was about as warm as a corpse when I showed up at seven a.m. for our first day working together. I had envisioned the staff being excited to have a new member on the team, especially someone who was so enthusiastic. But Monica *definitely* wasn't charmed by the latte I brought her from Dean & DeLuca. When I set it down on the desk and said, "Just a little something to kick off our first day working together!" she rolled her eyes and pointed to the back room. "Over there," she said, smacking gum between words. *Who chews gum at seven a.m.?*

I wasn't quite sure what she meant, so I proceeded as usual. "You want sugar in yours?"

Another eye roll. "No, you can't drink that up here. Company rules. Coffee and food in the back room only."

"Oh, it's fine," I said, shrugging. "Nobody is here yet anyway. Here, take yours."

"Don't act like you know the rules here. What's your name again?"

"I'm Liz."

"Well, *Liz*, there's a strict rule about no food at the desk. So if I were you, I'd take your coffees or lattes or whatever you brought, and put it in the back room like everyone else. Got it?"

I decided to take the not-so-subtle hint and walked the lattes to the back, leaving them on a counter next to a box of doughnuts and a can of Folgers. *I guess that's breakfast here?* I thought, a little queasy looking at the sad, greasy pastries, jelly oozing out of their middles. It's not that I didn't like sweets; I'd gone out the night before with Ben and some of our friends to celebrate . . . well, I'm not really sure what we were celebrating, but it was something. I'd meant to have a couple of drinks and be home by midnight, but a couple of glasses of champagne turned into a couple of shots, which turned into several cocktails, and before I knew it the sun was coming up and I was heading home for a shower and some sober-up coffee. *Ugh, I was counting on that latte*, I thought, wishing I had brought some Advil.

On my way back to the receptionist desk, I stopped in the restroom to do one last hair-makeup-wardrobe check before my meeting with Tony. My head might have been in a fog, but I didn't want him to know that. I smoothed out my hair, which was pulled back in a low ponytail, and checked my new black suit—I'd bought it off the rack in a panic the day before, because, Jesus, who owns a black suit?—for wrinkles. The suit was horrendous, so I paired it with beige suede Gucci heels and mabe pearl earrings. I thought back to the quote I picked for my high school yearbook; it was from *Sex and the City* and read, "Sometimes, the best you can do is play the hand you're dealt and accessorize the outfit that you're given." (I was super deep at eighteen.) Other than the bags under my eyes, and the heinous black hose I'd borrowed from my mom, I looked like a total pro. At the very least, I looked better than Monica, who had pulled her wet hair into a messy bun and was wearing some sort of sneaker-meets-dress-shoe that looked like it was dug out of the bargain bin at Payless. Although I did feel a little like Shelley Long in *Troop Beverly Hills* when she put on her scout-leader uniform for the first time. *Now if only I could get a designer to tailor this getup*, I thought.

Tony was supposed to give me a tour of the funeral

home—I'd been there for Dad's service, but I'd only seen the "front" of the place. The "back," a.k.a. the rooms that clients would never, ever be allowed to see, was all brand-new. But Tony was gearing up for a big wake that day, so instead, to my slight disappointment, he asked Monica to take me down to see Bill. "Tell her to wear her sweater, if she has one," he called out from the top of the stairs. Monica rolled her eyes. "Follow me," she said, as if she were being hugely inconvenienced.

I soon knew why Tony suggested a sweater: Monica walked me down to the embalming room, which is kept at a cool-ish sixty degrees and looks like a cross between a morgue and a dental office. I heard the faint sounds of what I thought was Bruce Springsteen humming from a stereo. "Bill's down there, he'll show you what you need to know," said Monica, wrapping her sweater tighter around her shoulders. "I'm going back up to the desk."

The smell of disinfectant seeped into my nostrils, and I felt my stomach flip-flop. *I guess this is where they keep the dead people?*

I took a few steps into the room to find Bill hunched over a dead body laid out on a stainless steel table. The body itself was covered in a white sheet, but Bill was perched over the head, applying concealer with a makeup sponge. "You're the new girl, I hear. Welcome to Crawford," he said. I recognized him as soon as he looked up—Bill had done Dad's touch-up just before the wake. Here he was again, adding some "life" to an otherwise pale face. I probably should have been freaked out by this, but instead, it felt strangely comforting to see the care Bill was taking with whoever's loved one was lying before him.

Bill stood up and showed me both of his hands, which were covered in latex gloves. He was tall, like Tony, but less round, and the same North Jersey accent rolled off his tongue. "You don't want me to shake your hand," he said. "I've got enough chemicals on these gloves to burn a hole through the floor." He pulled off the gloves and washed his hands in a small stainless steel sink that looked almost like a water fountain. "Let me just wash up, then I'll take you around. Oh, and welcome to the prep room! Most people are scared of this place, but if you're not one of them, come down whenever."

I laughed, relieved to be in friendly company after Monica's icy welcome. After Bill had taken off his white apron and put a black blazer on, we walked back upstairs. I'd already seen the six different view rooms available for wakes and funerals. They looked mostly like what you'd expect for a funeral home: formal, a little stuffy, with lots of ornate window treatments, old wallpaper, and prewar moldings. And just about every room had at least one chandelier. Bill told me he had been working at Crawford for almost thirty years. His dad, an Italian guy from North Jersey, had also been an embalmer. "It's just the family biz, you know?" he said, shuffling up a second flight of stairs. He pointed out the two main offices and then the back room that I had already seen. "You like Italian food? Wait till you eat lunch with us. We get all the good stuff, the galamad, the mutzarell, the braciole. We just order it and all eat it back here," he said, his accent really coming through. "You've got to eat mints after, though, or else you'll smell like garlic all day. My wife hates that."

I laughed.

"I guess better garlic than gangrene, though, right?" said Bill. "Wait until you get a whiff of *that*. It'll be your true test of whether you want to be in this industry." I was equal parts grossed out and fascinated.

After the half-hour tour, Bill went back down to the embalming room to finish up—but first he invited me on what was called a "removal." I didn't know exactly what that meant, but it sounded a lot better than sorting through folders at the desk.

"I just have to offer it to Monica first," he said. "As long as she passes, you can come."

"Oh, okay," I said, a little confused. *Why does he have to offer it to Monica?*

Bill must have read the look on my face. "The union, they pay an extra twenty-seven bucks for a removal," he said. "And union rules mean that I have to offer the gig to the person present with the most seniority.

"Hey, Mon, you want to do this removal with me?" said Bill.

Monica looked over at me and then back at Bill. If she went with him, I would be left in charge of the reception desk for the afternoon. "I'll pass," she said.

Bill raised his eyebrows at me and smiled. "Twenty-seven bucks, in your pocket!" he said. "I'll come get you a few minutes before it's time to go."

Monica was slowly looking through a folder when I sat back down next to her. "I'm excited to do a removal!" I said, as if she would possibly care.

"It's gross," said Monica. "You're going to freak." A small piece of me wondered if she was secretly hoping that the removal would be enough to scare me away from this place. A receptionist always had to go along with one of the guys to get a body—company rules. *Is this chick really willing to give up almost thirty dollars to get rid of me?* I thought. Just as I was about to ask what I should expect, Monica pointed to a stack of folders and asked if I had any plans of helping with them. The folders appeared to be in no particular order—just a mess of papers and invoices.

"So where are you from, anyway?" said Monica.

"I grew up right around the corner," I said, regretting it as soon as it came out of my mouth.

Monica raised her eyebrows, not in an *I'm impressed* kind of way, but more to convey, *I have already judged you up and down*. Which is exactly what she did, because the next thing I knew, she was staring at my shoes and mumbling something in her native tongue. To some extent, I understood: it didn't seem lost on her that I walked to work, while she and most of the other Crawford employees took hour-long subway rides, emerging in a different world on the other side. I had faith, at least then, that she would eventually come around and realize I wasn't the walking stereotype she assumed.

I was grateful when Bill came up from the basement a couple of boring, filing-heavy hours later holding a set of keys. "You ready?" he asked, already walking toward the door. I grabbed my coat and hurried after him, happy to get away from the desk—or more precisely, the ice queen behind it—and out into the fresh air. It was late March, but the cool sting of winter hadn't melted into spring yet.

Bill asked me to wait on the curb while he pulled up the van. It was pretty normal looking—just like any black minivan you'd see on the street, except the backseats had been taken out, replaced by a gurney. I hopped in the front seat, still unsure about what we were doing, and strapped on my seat belt.

"You a sports fan?" Bill asked as he steered the van south toward Seventy-Second Street.

"Huge Giants fan," I said. "So was my dad. We always get season tickets. Well, we did, anyway."

"Giants! Yes! I knew I liked you, Elizabeth," he said. Then, softening his voice, he added, "Hey, and I'm real sorry about your father. That was a beautiful service you put on for him. A beautiful service. I'd be proud if my kids did that for me."

Knowing that Bill had seen thousands of funerals, I was flattered that he remembered my dad's service. I didn't know what to say, so I just smiled as we crossed Central Park in the van, bouncing over potholes and speeding by taxis moving in the other direction. "So, before we get to where we're going, do I need to know anything?" I finally said.

"We are picking up a body," said Bill, like it was the most natural thing ever. "Sometimes when people die at home, we go get 'em at their apartments. It's not like their chauffeurs are going to bring them over."

Bill pulled the car up to the front of a fancy co-op on the Upper West Side and brushed off his blazer. I recognized the building—it was just a few blocks away from Trinity, the private school I'd attended as a teen. My head was pounding by this point, but I knew I couldn't focus on myself. We were about to enter someone's home, where his or her family would probably be gathered around, going through the same pain I'd gone through just weeks before. I took a deep breath and followed behind Bill. His whole demeanor changed the moment he stepped onto the sidewalk—gone was any sense of casualness. Instead, he walked up to the doorman with an aura of authority, and discreetly gave his name and the apartment number where we would be heading. He also let the doorman know what was about to happen. I listened carefully too (I was just as naïve as the doorman) as Bill explained that we were going to be taking a body out on a gurney, so it would be best if other residents of the building didn't have to witness the scene. Although he had placed a sign in the windshield, he also asked him to watch the van. The doorman listened intently, letting every one of Bill's words soak in so that he wouldn't mess up the grim procedure, and then stood out on the sidewalk to keep an eye on the van for us.

We didn't exchange a word the whole ride up to the penthouse, the two of us wedged on either side of the gurney in a freight elevator (normal elevators are too small). It was almost like a Method actor walking onto a set. There would be no breaking character. This was serious. Dead serious. My stomach dropped as the elevator went up, up, up. Bill might have been calm, but he was an old pro. I, on the other hand, was majorly nervous. What would we say to whoever was inside the apartment? Should I shake their hands hello? I'd been trained to know a social grace for every situation, but there wasn't exactly an Emily Post guide to picking up a dead body.

Bill slipped on a pair of white fabric gloves, like a waiter at a fine restaurant might wear, and a black hat that I didn't even realize he had been carrying with him. I felt like I should follow suit, so I fixed my pearl earrings to make sure the backs were on tight and pulled down the hem of my black blazer. My feet ached in my heels as we walked out of the elevator and onto the penthouse floor, which opened up into a mahogany and marble entry. Bill knocked lightly on the door, and moments later, a butler opened it. His eyes were red, like he had been crying, and behind him was a staff of at least ten people—maids, a chef, who knows who else—all with their heads hung low. Bill stood in front of the gurney, took off his hat, and simply said, "I am Bill from the funeral home, and this is my associate Elizabeth. Please accept our condolences. Would you mind directing us to the appropriate room?"

The butler led the way through the grand foyer and down a long, wide hallway. The apartment had the feel of a museum—grand and formal, perhaps like the person who lived there. My heels click-clacked down the hall until we entered a bedroom bigger than many New York City apartments, with ten-foot windows overlooking Central Park. Next to a four-poster bed was a hospital bed—they are commonly brought into homes during hospice care—and in that bed was an old man in blue herringbone pajamas. He looked peaceful, like he was still sleeping, and I instantly felt comforted by the reminder that death—at least the looks of it—wasn't nearly as scary as it was made out to be on TV and in movies. At least not for most people.

Bill went right to work pushing the gurney next to the bed and pulling out a body bag. He requested that the butler leave the room, because nobody should have to watch someone they knew and cared for be stuffed into a plastic bag. Once the coast was clear, Bill turned to me and said, "Okay, are you ready for this? It's a piece of cake. Lucky for you, you have the best possible teacher." I looked hard at

Bill as he rattled off the rest of the instructions: He would count to three, and then we'd hoist the sheet under the body, lifting the corpse into the bag that was already open on the gurney. Bill would hold the upper half, and I would take the legs. I felt nervous as I moved to the end of the bed and gripped the sheet, but I gave Bill an approving nod. There was no taking this back. I was doing this removal.

The man was heavier than he looked (the term "dead-weight" is no joke). My arms shook as I pulled up the lower corners of the sheet and shifted my weight from my left leg to my right. It was a relief to have the body safely in one piece, on the gurney, ready for transport. I was feeling pretty awesome about successfully completing my first removal, when I looked down at my feet. My $600 Gucci heels, the suede ones that Monica had scoffed at earlier in the day, were *covered* in a brownish fluid.

"Oh my God," I said, lifting up my left foot.

Bill surveyed the damage and shrugged. "Gotta watch out for that. They leak," he said, before putting his hat back on and leading the gurney out the door.

The doorman was waiting for us in the lobby and gave us the go-ahead so that we could move through with as few people seeing as possible. Bill wheeled the gurney, body bag on top, onto a platform on the back of the van, which lifted with a flip of a switch. Then he closed the doors, slipped off the gloves, and got back in the driver's seat. I was still sulking about my shoes on the inside, but I badly wanted to impress Bill now that I had seen him in action and wouldn't dare complain.

On the ride back to Crawford, I heard a *thud-thud-thud* sound coming from the back of the van. I felt like the guy we had just picked up, a little blue in the face and dripping God knows what fluids from orifices I was trying to block from my mind, was knocking at us, like, *Hey, assholes, the least you could have done is strap me in.*

"What *is* that?" I asked, the *thud* sound ringing louder and louder as we drove back over the potholes. I looked down at my stained shoes and wondered if this whole thing was maybe a big, messy mistake.

"That?" Bill said, pointing behind him.

I nodded.

"The gurney bangs up against the divider," he said with a shrug. "Don't worry, you'll get used to it."

BY THE TIME I got back to my apartment that night, I was too tired to make dinner, so I pulled a pint of chocolate froyo out of the freezer and collapsed onto my couch. My whole body hurt—never again would I wear designer heels to work—and I decided that maybe Monica had the right idea with her old-lady comfort shoes.

I heard my phone vibrate, and a text from Gaby popped up: HEY! IF YOU'RE TOO BUSY TO BOOK YOUR FLIGHT TO LON-DON, I'M MORE THAN HAPPY TO DO IT FOR YOU.

London. Ugh. I hated to let my best friend down, but there was no way I could go to the party. Monica had made the schedule for the week, and since I was the newbie, I got all the worst shifts—my days were going to be starting at either six a.m. or four p.m., and it wasn't going to be pretty. Plus, I had to work weekends.

I dipped my spoon deep into the froyo and picked up my phone. SO SORRY HUN BUT I THINK I HAVE TO WORK.

Buzzzz. BUT YOU CAN'T MISS THIS PARTY!! PRETTY PLEASE?? DON'T MAKE ME GO WITHOUT YOU. CAN'T YOU JUST TELL YOUR BOSS YOU HAVE PLANS OR SOMETHING?

Just as I was about to write back, Elaine's name popped up on my phone. *Why in God's name is she calling me?* I thought. Don't get me wrong—Elaine did the obligatory check-in call from time to time, usually to ask how "our" fabulous friends were doing. But she spoke to Max much more than me, and even when we did connect, it always felt a little awkward, like when you're sitting next to someone at a party who is four drinks deeper than you.

I'm not going to answer it. She is just going to say something stupid, and I'll hate her for it. I hit "ignore" and reached for the TV remote, but her name started flashing again. (Elaine does not like to be ignored.)

"Yes, hi, Nanny," I said, not even attempting to sound happy to hear from her. "What can I do for you?"

"Lizzie, oh good, you're there. I talked to your brother. What is this I hear about you working at a funeral home? I know this couldn't possibly be the case, but I wanted to hear it from you."

Sigh. My new gig might have been a disappointment for my mother, but it would be an outright embarrassment for Elaine, a woman so "refined" she refused to let her staff pour her milk straight out of a carton into her coffee. They had to pour the milk into a silver pitcher first, *then* pour it into Elaine's coffee or whatever Nanny Dearest was drinking.

"Nanny, I'm tired. I really don't feel like getting into this with you," I said.

"Well, I didn't ask you how you *feel*, Lizzie. You need to stop this foolishness. I know you're upset that your father isn't here anymore, but this isn't the way a lady *deals with things*. You hear me? Can't you go out with your girlfriends or something? What's my Gaby up to these days? Why don't you both come down for a visit?"

A text from Gaby buzzed through. HELLO? OKAY, I'M COUNTING YOU IN. LONDON! PARTY! YAY!

My head was pounding. Why didn't anyone in my life understand that this wasn't a joke? "Elaine . . . er, Nanny . . . I've—I've got to go," I said, hanging up the phone before she could respond.

I looked at the clock: seven p.m. Normally I'd be making plans to meet friends in the Meatpacking District, or maybe for dinner in the East Village. But I had eleven precious hours before I'd be sitting at the reception desk at Crawford, and the thought of putting on a cute dress, cabbing it downtown, and squeezing myself into a booth next to a bunch of friends fresh from happy hour was about as appealing as whatever brown liquid had oozed onto my shoes earlier. I turned off my phone. The only thing calling my name for the rest of the night was a pair of cashmere sweatpants, an oversized T-shirt, and a bottle of water.

Besides, just about the last thing I needed was for someone else to ask me what the hell I was doing with my life, when I barely knew myself.

THREE

Dirty Business

*W*hen I was seven, my parents signed me up for ballet lessons. Or rather, my mother signed me up—Dad had nothing to do with it. Mom bought me a pair of leather Capezio dance slippers, white tights, a pink leotard . . . and a tutu. I may not have been savvy in the ways of my mom's and Elaine's persuasion tactics just yet, but I was smart enough to know that this did not bode well for my afternoons playing soccer in the park. So I refused to dance, instead standing there with the tutu on my head while all the other little girls pranced around the Madison Avenue dance studio, their wispy buns bobbing up and down while their nannies looked on. Mom was too embarrassed to bring me back after that—are you sensing a theme?—and so she let me play with my brother and his friends in Central Park, with scraped knees and grass stains on our shorts. I guess what I'm trying to say is: I've never been afraid to get a little messy.

That might be one of the reasons why after four months working at Crawford, I started to find myself less and less at the front desk with Monica, and more and more downstairs in the embalming room with Bill. Not only could he talk about the chances of the Giants winning that Sunday, he also didn't make fun of me in Spanish. (I'd picked up enough since I started to know that "*perra rica*" meant "rich bitch.") Plus, it turned out that Bill was the Monet of the funeral business. Everyone who dealt with death knew him, or at least knew *of* him. Not to sound crass, but he could take the victim of a drunk driving accident, face all bashed in, and make him look so good, you'd think he was going to a five-star dinner at Daniel. Seriously, Bill was that good.

I looked on in amazement the first time I saw Bill prep a body in his immaculate prep room—it was by far the cleanest area in the whole funeral home. First, he looked at the folder to make sure he had gone through every one of the family's wishes and knew them by heart. People could be very particular about how a loved one should look—they'd request a certain shade of lipstick (sometimes they'd even drop it off) or hairstyle, specify how jewelry should be arranged. Bill listened to all of it. "Funerals aren't so much for the dead as they are for the living," he said, busy at work. "You know, one last chance for friends and family to see that face, those hands." And so, he made it his mission to see that *that* face and *those* hands looked just like when the person was alive. More, and this is particularly true for people who battled with long illnesses (chemo made people lose their hair, steroids left bodies bloated, liver failure caused jaundice), he made them look alive and *well*.

After reading through the family's requests, Bill would then do something very important: he made sure the person lying on that stainless steel table was actually dead, either by checking for a pulse or holding a mirror under the nose to make sure it didn't fog up. I know, this sounds completely crazy, but early in his career, Bill started working on a body and it accidentally slipped off the stretcher. (This almost never happened, but it could.) When he went to pick the body up, he saw that blood was gushing from the head—a sign of a beating heart, which any well-behaved corpse doesn't have. "I lost my shit," said Bill, recounting the moment with a slight smile. "Started screaming to the guys upstairs, 'Call 911! He's alive!' And I think for a moment they thought I'd gone off the deep end. For a second, *I* thought I'd gone off the deep end. But hey, at least the guy got to live, right? Better to have a bad bruise on your head than to be dead."

When it was actually time to work on the body, he'd retrieve it from one of the freezers, where bodies were kept cold on three slats. (Back in the day, Bill said that they literally kept the bodies on ice; the guys on staff also kept their beers cool in the freezer, sticking them around the corpses.

Ew!) He then transferred the body to one of the tables. The corpses were always respectfully covered, with just the part Bill was working on exposed. He was covered too—usually a long white coat with an apron on top, shoe covers, and gloves. The first part of body prep was to loosen up any rigor mortis that had set in by bending the arms and legs. Then he set the features, which meant slipping plastic caps under both eyelids to avoid a sunken-in look (eyeballs can sink back into the head after death) and closing the lids over them. The mouth was wired shut using small needles attached to metal wires. Next up: embalming. Like a surgeon, Bill cut a slit on the lower part of the body's neck near the collarbone and drained out the blood through tubes inserted in the arteries, only to replace it with a pink-ish embalming fluid that brought color to the skin. You know those pretty pink cheeks you see at wakes? All smoke and mirrors. Or rather, dye and chemicals.

While the blood was being replaced by embalming fluid (the blood simply went down the sink drain as it flowed out), Bill washed the body with a sponge, which was less about cleaning and more about making sure that all the embalming fluid was getting distributed. Then he whipped out a trocar, which looks like a metal pencil with a really long, pointy tip attached to a suction tube, and inserted it in the abdomen to release any other bodily fluids and gases still hanging around. That part wasn't my favorite, I'll admit. But then again, wouldn't you be kind of creeped out if it were?

Finally, Bill would switch gears from surgeon to beautician. The man had a whole makeup station in the embalming room, filled mostly with special products meant to be used on cold, stiff skin. But there were also Essie nail polishes, Chanel lipsticks, hair extensions, and more blushes than the Saks makeup counter had, all left over from families who had dropped off their loved ones' beauty kits and never picked them up. Bill was also diligent about restocking the essentials, like fake eyelashes. He was a master at curling waves, covering gray roots, and trimming bangs, and he knew more beauty secrets than the glossy women's magazines. I swear, he gave better manicures than the ladies at the nail salon next door.

One night, I was heading out for an event and had changed into my velvet Roberto Cavalli gown at the office. The only hiccup: the dress was low-cut, and I had forgotten my boob tape. "Hold on, I got something even better," Bill said. Then he pulled wig tape out of a drawer and told me to stick it wherever things were "jiggling around." It worked better than any fashion tape, and from then on, I took all of my grooming advice from a middle-aged man who chain-smoked and spent most of his days around dead bodies.

"IF YOU'RE GOING to keep hanging out down here, you better put some gloves on," Bill said one morning, tossing a box filled with white latex my way. Between the smell of disinfectant from the cleaning supplies, the formaldehyde in the embalming fluid, and that powdery, plasticky latex odor, you'd think this would be the last place I'd want to be. But Bill seemed to know *everything* about the funeral business, and I couldn't get enough. Plus, he played much better music than the instrumental string shit always streaming through the lobby.

"Oh, I probably don't need them," I said, putting the box down.

"You wanna catch something? Put the gloves on," said Bill, pointing at the box.

"What am I going to catch from a dead person?"

Bill sighed. "You ever hear of Creutzfeldt-Jakob disease, kid?"

I shook my head.

"Of course you haven't. Now put the gloves on."

I did as Bill said, not only because I wanted to stay in the embalming room, but also because I didn't want to catch whatever he was talking about. I'm going to go out on a limb here and guess that you've never heard of Creutzfeldt-Jakob disease, either. (Or maybe you have, in which case you probably hang out with an even quirkier crowd than I do.) Embalmers are terrified of it, and you would be too if you spent your days cutting open dead people and touching their brains—which is exactly how it's transmitted. CJD is a rare brain disease that causes sudden dementia and other problems like seizures, jerky movements, and psychosis. Most people who get it are dead within a year, and while CJD isn't a big risk for most of the population (the Department of Health reports about twenty-two cases a year in New York), embalmers are particularly at risk because they can be exposed to contaminated brain tissue. How someone hasn't made a zombie movie about this is beyond me.

"Kinda crazy that dead people can kill you, huh?" said Bill.

He also introduced me to tissue gas, which builds up in dead bodies and creates a sort of crinkling Rice Krispies sound. It takes a few hours for all the gases to work their way out, which isn't dangerous or toxic, but a little stomach-turning to think about. "Snap, crackle, pop!" Bill said, and I couldn't help but laugh. Sure, it was a little gross—but I also found myself surprisingly curious about what, exactly, happened to bodies after death. Like most people, I'd thought a lot about where our souls might go. The decomposing corpse? Not so much.

YOU'D THINK that Tony would have been annoyed I was spending so much time downstairs, but he was usually too busy trying to woo customers into buying overpriced crap they didn't need to even notice where I was. I'd caught a glimpse of his salesmanship when I came in to arrange Dad's funeral, but that was nothing compared to the show he put on for the families of celebrities, politicians, or anyone whose name he recognized from the *New York Post*. Tony was a classic up-seller: he knew that if someone could afford to have their loved one laid to rest at Crawford, they could probably afford a pricier casket and anything else he threw at them. And since most people who came into Crawford were in a daze of grief, they were usually not in the mood to protest about prices. "Here's my AmEx," they'd say, tossing their platinum credit cards across the desk. "Just make it nice." In my opinion, Tony was sometimes a little *too* happy to oblige, but I was glad to be learning about the business in such a hands-on way.

Even though Monica didn't like my sitting with her at the reception desk, she seemed even more annoyed that I was getting special privileges, like being allowed to tell florists where to put flowers, going on removals, and of course spending time with Bill and learning the business. It's not that anyone told me to do these things; it's just that nobody protested when I did. And after practically growing up planning parties and events—if there's one thing you learn living in Manhattan, it's how to throw a killer fête—it felt natural to jump in and help make sure the prayer cards were stacked right, the paintings were level, the candy dishes were filled with upscale chocolates, and there weren't any stray petals on the floor. My years of attending charity dinners and other fancy events had taught me that the details mattered—and so did the attitude of the staff. I *cared* what the clients thought, and that they felt taken care of.

Monica, on the other hand, was mostly worried about scheduling the calendar so that I didn't have one Saturday or Sunday off, and monitoring my breaks to make sure I never came in a second after my thirty minutes were up. (I didn't. I wasn't going to give her the satisfaction of scolding me in front of the other staff members.) She might as well have been working at the checkout in a grocery store for all the attention she paid to client satisfaction.

I'd been going in and out of the embalming room for a few days when Bill called me to come down again. "Do you have the folder for the body that was just brought in?" he asked when I walked into the chilly room. I wasn't on phones that morning, so I had no idea where the folder might be—although the stack of messy papers in front of where Monica had been sitting was one possibility. The folders were supposed to be stored in an area along the wall behind the desk that functioned like a library; only funeral directors were to grab them, and then return them promptly after use.

"Hold on, let me check," I said, already walking back up the stairs. After a couple of minutes of sifting through papers at the reception desk, I still didn't see anything, so I called down to the prep room. "Let me ring you in a minute, I need to ask Tony about this," I told Bill.

He sighed into the phone. "Okay," he said. "I'll just be down here with the body."

I found Tony sitting in his office, flipping through his

Rolodex. "Bill's looking for the folder for the body that was just brought in," I said.

Tony looked up. "The AIDS guy?"

"Uh, I don't . . . I don't know about that," I said, surprised. "Just whoever was brought in this morning."

"That's the AIDS guy," said Tony. "Some of the boys have been trying to figure out all morning if he's gay or if it was a drug thing. You know, needles or whatever." I was shocked at their attitude—like it was 1984 and everyone thought only gay people got AIDS.

"I'm not sure that's really relevant," I said, suddenly wondering about who this person might have been, what his life was like. "I'm just looking for the notes."

After a few minutes of digging around his desk, Tony plucked the folder from underneath his planner and shook his head. "Monica must have left it in here," he said, handing it over. He paused for a moment. "What were you doing in the prep room?"

"Oh, uh, I thought I should learn how all parts of the funeral process work," I said, hoping he wouldn't be mad.

Tony gave me a puzzled look before breaking out in a slight smile. "A go-getter, eh?" he said, shaking his head. "Well, this is new. All right, go. Go on."

When I got to the basement, Bill was already done up in his apron and gloves, and he was looking through a stack of CDs next to a small black stereo that still had the Radio-Shack sticker on it. "I gotta put some Bruce on," he said.

That's when I saw the body, already laid out on the table. I took a closer peek and rolled my eyes. The guy had a waxed chest, highlighted hair, and two pierced ears. Either he was gay, or Ryan Seacrest had died and nobody had noticed yet.

"I haven't seen an AIDS case in a while," Bill said, Bruce Springsteen's *Darkness on the Edge of Town* album buzzing through the speakers. "Always brings me down a little. Reminds me of the eighties." I vaguely remembered people wearing red ribbons when I was a kid, but it felt like a faraway, adult problem. By the time my friends and I actually understood what AIDS was, most of the panic was over. My college friends and I were much more concerned with catching herpes than contracting HIV.

My heart sank listening to Bill talk about the AIDS epidemic that swept through New York City starting in 1981. Nobody understood how the mysterious disease was being transmitted or what was causing it. Embalmers had been terrified. "They said you could get it through contact with bodily fluids," Bill told me, shaking his head. "And I'm here thinking, *I deal with those every day*. It wasn't as clear then that there had to be a little, you know, a little more involved than that."

Crawford had an unexpected boom in business during the 1980s. "Every day, there were at least a few bodies, if not more," said Bill. "Young guys, so thin, and the bodies, they just kept coming. It was terrible. I mean, good for business, but that didn't even matter—it was awful to see. And I was a young guy myself, then, and I'm just looking at these bodies, and it seemed so crazy that nobody could help these guys, you know?" He shook his head and lowered his voice. "Nobody could help them."

Springsteen's "Badlands" came on, and neither Bill nor I said anything as he returned his attention to the body on the table, but I wondered if he noticed the all-too-true lyrics as much as I did: "It ain't no sin to be glad you're alive." They reminded me of something my dad would have said. Of course, Dad was more Stones than Springsteen, but I think he would have agreed with the sentiment.

AFTER WORKING six days straight, I finally had a day off. For a second, I thought I had dozed off in the funeral home; I woke up next to two four-foot-wide floral arrangements that I had taken home from a service the night before. People spent thousands, sometimes tens of thousands, of dollars on roses and orchids and hydrangeas for services, and then every night, we were left to toss them into garbage bags and throw them in the Dumpster out back. It seemed like such a waste, so I started bringing the prettier arrangements home. What? *Somebody* should enjoy them.

I was jolted out of my sleepy state by the sound of my phone ringing.

"Hello?" I said, trying not to sound as groggy as I felt.

"Almost ready?" said Gaby. She was working on a series

of paintings at the time, and so she was available to hang out on a random Tuesday. Although to be fair, a lot of our friends had what you might call "leisurely" schedules.

I looked at my alarm clock, which I hadn't set. It was already eleven a.m.

"Uh, kind of," I said.

"You're totally still in bed!" said Gaby, laughing. "Get up! Get up, get up, get up! You get to hang out with a living person today! Should we hit up Bergdorf's?"

"Meh, maybe we just go with the usual," I said. What I really needed was a new pair of comfortable shoes. Monica may have been a nightmare to work with, but the woman knew how to keep her feet from throbbing—I'd been wearing old-lady flats to work for weeks. I also wanted to pick up another off-the-rack suit or two. I already had three black suits I wouldn't be caught *dead* in outside of work hanging next to the Armani gowns in my closet, but adding a few more to the rotation would mean fewer trips to the dry cleaners.

"Okay, okay. Fine. I'm just happy to see you finally," said Gaby. "I still can't believe you missed London! I have to show you the pics. You'll die."

I met Gaby on the corner of Madison and Seventy-Second. It was our usual spot, since I liked to start off any shopping trip with a stroll through Ralph Lauren, where most of the salespeople knew me by name. Plus it was near Via Quadronno, our favorite lunch spot, which had the *best* cappuccinos in the city. I could see Gaby from a block away—she was dressed in her daytime regulars, which included a baggy tank top, big sunglasses, and pants that most women could barely squeeze their arms into. I always told her that the trade-off for having such a crazy family was that, good Lord, she at least got fabulous genes out of the deal.

"Hi, hi, hi!" I said, skipping toward her. Before I'd started working at Crawford, we'd hung out almost every day—now I was lucky to see her once a week.

Gaby gave me a hug and pointed at the store behind us. "Shall we?" she said.

"I was actually hoping we could hit up the Aerosoles store," I said. Gaby might have grown up wealthy, but she wasn't a clothing snob.

She shook her head and laughed. "Your mom would freak if she found out you were walking around in those."

I laughed too—it felt good to have a conversation that didn't take place in front of a corpse. "Oh, totally. Although, I haven't even talked to Mom in a few days. She wanted me to go to the country house last weekend, but I couldn't make it with work."

"How's she doing?" said Gaby.

"She's hanging in there," I said.

"Have you two been talking about your dad? Maybe it would be good for both of you to . . ."

"It's hard," I said. "Dad was always my person, you know? Mom and Max, Dad and me. I want to connect with her, but she's so against me working at Crawford, and I don't know how to make her understand it."

"Maybe she doesn't have to understand it right now," said Gaby. "Remember when you wanted to go to NYU and she didn't understand why you couldn't just go to Tufts like Max? She eventually came around."

I could feel my chest tighten up. I *wanted* things to be easier with my mom. We both just felt so . . . off. I kept telling myself that we just needed some time to make everything feel normal again, or at least as normal as it could be without Dad around.

"Maybe," I said, my voice softening.

We walked in silence for another few minutes—something we *never* did. Then Gaby said, "What do you think happens when you die?"

"Well, first they take your body away, and then once it's at the funeral home, they make this small incision—"

"Oh my God, no! No no! Stop, that's so disgusting," said Gaby. "I mean what do you think happens to your *spirit*?"

I was quiet again. I wasn't particularly religious, and yet I wanted to believe that Dad was *somewhere* other than inside the urn my mom had placed on her bedroom shelf. It was terrifying to think about. What if I made sense of it all and came up with an answer I didn't like? Then what? My mind flashed to Bill the day before, hunched over a body, gluing on eyelashes and plumping up cheeks. The body itself had a peaceful look, and I was satisfied knowing that we had seen this person through to the end of *this* world. But I realized then that I'd never let myself think beyond that.

"Ah, puppies!" Gaby said, breaking my train of thought. We were about to walk by a pet store that always had little Pomeranians and King Charles spaniels in the window. Gaby might have been the only person I knew who loved dogs even more than I did.

I followed her to the window, happy that a bunch of furry balls of cuteness had let me off the hook from answering her question. But even as we stood there cooing at the dogs, I started to feel an uneasy knot in my stomach: *Where do we go when we're no longer here?* I thought about the bodies on Bill's metal embalming tables and where, if anywhere, their souls were at that moment. I could imagine them floating around us, popping in and out of our world and some other realm as they pleased. I wanted to believe that—if not for my dad, for myself.

FOUR

We've Lost Her Mind

*L*ovey girl, it's Nanny. I'm flying up to New York next week with the Smirnoffs. I hope my granddaughter can take an hour away from death to see the old lady. If not, then I'll see you at *my* funeral, I suppose. Although you'll have to drink alone then."

Even through voice mail, the woman could lay on a guilt trip.

Elaine had been raised uptown, like me. She went to finishing school instead of earning a college degree, the best option for wealthy girls at the time. To be fair, this wasn't abnormal in the 1940s—but I still cringed imagining her curtsying and actually *learning* to be charming. Her whole life was filled with silly rituals like this, and she was constantly being taken care of: First, an army of nannies and chauffeurs and maids (oh my!) watched over her while her parents went to parties dressed in furs. After that, it was a husband. When he died of a heart attack, there was *another* husband she somehow lined up for the role. I have no idea how Elaine managed to land so many men, but I will say this: the woman wasn't about to let one guy's failed organ hold her back from winters in Palm Beach and summers cruising on the *Queen Elizabeth II*.

I hid my phone back in my pocket and picked up Crawford's line, which had been ringing off the hook all morning. *What is it with today?* I thought, holding the receiver up to my ear.

"Crawford Funeral Home. How may I direct your call?" I said.

"Yes. Hello," said a nervous-sounding man on the other end of the line. "Tony, please. My mother was brought in this morning. I have a favor to ask."

Tony was gone for the morning, and I knew he wouldn't be back for hours. "I'm sorry to hear about your mother," I said. "Tony's not available at the moment. I'm his . . . uh . . . how can I help you?"

"I need . . . my sister and I . . . *we* need . . . Can you tell me that my mother's brain is in her head?"

Come again? I thought.

"Her name—it's Annie. Can you check for me? I need to know absolutely for certain that it's in there."

"Not a problem, sir. Let me check in on this and call you back in just a few minutes," I said.

"I'll hold."

I raced down to the embalming room to find Bill.

"Liz!" he said. "You see the game last night? What were our boys doing out there? We've got to work on defense or we don't have a shot in hell at—"

"We can't talk Giants right now," I said, a little out of breath from running so fast. (My crazy work schedule wasn't leaving much time for my usual morning jogs in Central Park.) "There's a guy on the phone, and he says we need to make sure that his mom's brain is still in her head. Does that make any sense?"

"What's her name?" said Bill.

"Annie something," I said. "She came in this morning."

Bill picked up a piece of paper and scanned it. "Yup, here's her paperwork," he said.

I walked over to see what he was holding. It looked like an autopsy report, and there was a list of all organs still inside of the body, right there: liver, lungs, brain . . .

"Bingo!" said Bill.

Before I could thank him, I was running back up to the front desk. "Hello? Are you still there?"

"Still here," said the man. "So is everything where it should be?"

"Yes, the autopsy report says that the brain is—"

"No, no, no. Not the autopsy report. I need somebody to tell me *for certain* that the brain is there. It's very important."

"Well, the report says—"

"You're not listening to me. I need you to physically *see* the brain."

Am I hearing this right? I thought. "Of course, sir," I said. "It may take a moment to accomplish what you're asking. Would you like me to call you ba—"

"I'll hold," he said.

Bill was working on another body when I raced back into the embalming room. "I don't know what to do," I told him. "He wants us to see the brain."

Bill sighed. "It's on the fucking sheet."

"I know, I know it's on the sheet. But he said it's important. Maybe she was, like, murdered, or something." Just as I said it, something clicked in my brain: Annie. Murder. *No fucking way*, I thought. "Bill, give me that sheet for a sec?"

Sure enough, there was her name: Annie Nast. The woman was the stuff of New York City legend. She grew up in Manhattan around the same time as Elaine—but with the kind of money that set her in a whole other class. Annie was the daughter of a businessman, and when he died when she was just a girl, she inherited tens of millions of dollars. It's an outrageous amount of money now, but it was downright *absurd* at the time. To top it off, she was beautiful—she looked like she could have been sisters with Grace Kelly. And they had similar taste in men, because, like Grace, Annie married a prince. They divorced after two kids and almost a decade of marriage, but still, *the woman married a prince*. And when the whole thing ended, she actually wound up paying *him* a settlement of a million dollars, plus a couple of estates. Baller move, especially back in the day, when most women still relied on husbands to pay their bills.

Annie's biggest downfall might have been her crappy taste in men. She was still pretty, and Lord knows she was still rich, when she found herself back on the market, and it didn't take her long to find husband number two. On the social scale, this guy was a significant downgrade—I mean, where do you go after a prince, really? Despite what people might have said, Annie went ahead and married Frederick Nast. The next thing you knew, they had a kid. You would have thought things were pretty good. This guy would have been straight-up mental to stray on his gorgeous sugar mama. But like many men with an inferiority complex, ol' Frederick had a mistress before they'd been married very long. Nobody knew if things were ever that great between him and Annie anyway, but pretty much *everyone* knew it by the time they were on the brink of divorce. (It didn't help that they would talk openly about it at parties. Total faux pas.)

Before you could say "divorce papers," Annie was suddenly and inexplicably in a coma. And not one of those Sandra Bullock–movie, my-lipstick-is-still-perfect-even-though-I've-been-unconscious-for-two-days comas, but one that lasted for *decades*. All fingers pointed toward Frederick. Blabbing about how much you hate your wife is never a smart precursor to killing her, especially when there's serious cash on the line. Neither is having your mistress take the stand at your murder trial to reveal that she had given you an ultimatum to leave your wife. But you couldn't just *leave her*—good God, no—because a divorce would cut you off from her fortune. Frederick was convicted but quickly teamed up with a big-shot lawyer for his appeal. In a second trial, Frederick's guilty verdict was overturned after the defense called up one medical expert after another who claimed Annie wasn't killed by her greedy shit of a husband but rather her own form of self-medication.

The upper crust of New York watched the trials like it was *Days of Our Lives*. It was the 1980s. The city was hot with co-caine, crime, and more money than it knew what to do with. (So I've read. I was, like, two. My New York was filled with car-ousel rides in Central Park and My Little Ponies.) Finally, at the request of Annie's two children from her previous marriage, Frederick agreed to grant Annie—still in her coma—a divorce and leave the country. She eventually ended up in a nursing home, kept alive by machines, and allegedly never with a blip of brain activity, until she died as an old lady. Heartbreaking.

And now here she was at Crawford. "Bill," I said, "you know who this is, right?" There had been books written, even movies made about Annie's murder trial. People couldn't resist the juicy plotline. It was like reality TV before there was even a name for it.

Bill looked at the sheet again. He might not have lived in Manhattan—none of the other Crawford staff did—but he'd certainly seen the news reports all those years ago. "I'll be damned," he said.

The only way to see what, exactly, was left of Annie was to cut open her skull. Bill started to cut with extreme precision while I braced myself for an eyeful of brains. I even held my gloved hands out to make sure that nothing fell on the floor. Finally, there was enough of an opening to see inside.

That's when the paper towels fell out.

They unfolded like an accordion—pieces of Bounty that had been stuffed in there in place of what we were *actually* looking for. "Oh my God!" I said, my heart racing.

"Take it easy, take it easy," said Bill, his voice steady. He scratched his head and shrugged. "It might be in her stomach."

"Her *stomach*? Why would her brain be in her stomach?"

"Sometimes after an autopsy, they take all the organs and stick 'em in a bag, then sew it up in the stomach," said Bill.

I raised my eyebrows.

"It's just what they do," he said. "I don't make the rules."

It all sounded very Egyptian to me, but it's not like I had any better ideas. I looked on as Bill undid the Y-shaped stitches in her abdomen and pulled out a bag—no joke, like a plastic bag—filled with organs. Bill laid them all out on the table, and I stared at the pieces, trying to figure out which was which. Biology was never my best subject, but after a quick scan, I was pretty sure our worst fears were realized: there was no brain. I felt a wave of anxiety. I was going to have to go back upstairs, pick up the phone, and tell Annie's son that we had no idea where his mother's brain went. I tried to imagine the conversation:

"Hello again! It's Elizabeth. So, now, here's a funny story, I mean you're really going to get a hoot out of this. We can't find the brain! It totally vanished! We thought it would be . . . you know . . . IN HER HEAD. But it's not. Ha! Anyway, it's okay, because I got you a free roll of paper towels out of the deal . . ."

I snapped back into the present. "What am I supposed to tell her son?" I asked Bill, a jolt of panic running through me. This was a *big* problem. Things had been going so *well* at Crawford. Thanks to all the extra hours I worked and my connection with clients, Tony had started to treat me more as a funeral planner than a receptionist, and I was allowed to do more than answer phones all day—the task I was actually hired for. *I can't do this, I can't do this, I can't do this*, I thought. I started longing for my apartment and a nice bottle of wine. In my old life, the one before Crawford, murder mysteries were never on the menu.

When I got back to my desk, I took a deep breath and picked up the phone. Another of my dad's sayings popped into my head: "Sometimes there's no way out but through."

So through I would go. "Hello, sir, are you still there?" I said, feeling slightly queasy. (And not from a hangover this time.)

"Elizabeth. Here. Yes. Did you find it?" he said.

Deep breath. "I'm sorry to relay this news, but we actually weren't able to locate the brain. Or, rather, we looked . . . but it's . . . it's—it's not there, sir."

"That's what I needed to know. Thank you," he said. Then, before I could say another word: *click*. He hung up.

What just happened? I thought.

I never heard about the brain again—not at Crawford, not in the newspapers or *Vanity Fair*, which had covered Annie's death at length. I wondered if they wanted the brain to test it for chemicals—maybe one last-ditch effort to prove their mom (the "kids," of course then adults, still called her "Mummy") had been murdered. Instead, Annie was prepped and brought to a church on Park Avenue for an impressive funeral. Almost all the pews were filled. A choir sang. Her son gave a eulogy that touched on everything from his mummy's amazing taste in design and affinity for cute dogs (she'd had four, before the coma) to her hidden dream of being an astronaut. Afterward, they held a reception in a grand space on Fifth Avenue, where Annie's friends—now old—ate cucumber sandwiches and sipped champagne in her honor. Perhaps her kids let the murder thing go; proving Frederick guilty wasn't going to bring their mother back. But it was hard not to feel like there was something unfinished about the whole thing.

When I got back to my apartment that night, I had an urgent feeling that I needed to see my mom. Max had told me the day before that she was doing fine—she was mostly busying herself with learning about investing, since Dad had always taken care of that—but that was about as much detail as he gave me. I kicked off my Aerosoles and hung up my Ann Taylor black blazer; changed into jeans, a button-down, and a string of pearls; and called her, thinking of those kids, who'd been grieving their mother for decades.

"Hello, Elizabeth," she said, sounding exhausted.

"I'm on my way over," I said. "Is that okay?"

It was quiet for a moment. "You know you don't need to ask if you can come home."

Maggie greeted me at the door the way she always did, by barreling into me and slapping my legs with her tail. I pet her ears and gave her a kiss, wishing that I could bring her home with me—but I knew my mother needed her. Still, it was so much easier greeting the dog than my mom, who was standing in the foyer with a cashmere shawl wrapped around her. I was startled by how much weight she had lost. Dad's death had stressed us all to our limits, but Mom looked frailer than I'd remembered.

"Hi," I said softly, walking toward her. I gave her a hug. "How are you?"

Mom nodded her head. "I'm fine," she said. She was always so strong, stronger than she needed to be.

We made a pot of Earl Grey tea and a plate of cookies and sat down in the den. The apartment had a sadness hanging in it—I could actually feel my dad's *not* being there, like a cloud hanging over the place. I imagined my mom alone in this space, night after night, and felt a pang of guilt.

"Have you been going out with friends at all?" I asked. I hated to think of her here by herself.

Mom shrugged. "Sometimes. They're starting to drop off," she said.

"Drop off? What do you mean?" I asked.

"All of our friends, your father's and mine, they're all couples. We hung out in couples. Well, I'm not a couple anymore. It throws the whole thing off balance, I guess."

"Not the Bergers though, right?" I said. The Bergers lived two floors down and had been close friends of my parents for over a decade.

"Oh, don't be mad at them, this is just what happens," said Mom. "At first, people come over all the time and they call you to get coffee or dinner. But after a month goes by, they just . . . move on. And they feel . . . I don't know, weird, I guess, inviting me now. They don't want me to be the third wheel. Or the fifth. Or the seventh. Odd numbers are far less comfortable than evens."

"Yeah, but do they have to do everything with their husbands?" I said. I couldn't imagine Gaby and me abandoning each other like that.

"You don't have to worry about me," said Mom, touching my hand. "I'm worried about you. This funeral thing. Isn't it time to do something else?"

I pulled my hand away, annoyed that she couldn't see that I was helping people . . . and myself. Planning funerals was the one thing that was keeping me sane.

"It's not some hobby," I said. "This is my *job*. Besides, I like it. I'm helping people."

Maggie waddled over to the table and sat between my feet, hoping for a stray crumb. Sadly for her, neither Mom nor I had touched the cookies. I thought about Annie and her love for dogs. I felt so much loss for her and the life she didn't get to finish. What might she have done in those lost years, had she not been a body in a bed?

"Elizabeth, are you listening to me?" said Mom, now looking slightly annoyed. "You're staring into space."

"Sorry," I said, snapping out of it. "What did you say again?"

Mom sighed. "It's like you choose what you want to hear," she said. She took a sip of her tea. "I just think it's time you thought about your next move. People are starting to talk . . ."

"Oh, okay, and I should care about what a bunch of stuffy women think, rather than living my own life?" I said.

"Would you just stop?" said Mom. "Why do you always have to do the opposite of everyone else? Look at your brother. He's a lawyer. He has a girlfriend. He's traveling to interesting places. Do you want to spend some of the best years of your life locked in a death home with corpses and crying people? Life isn't long, Elizabeth. It's not. I just hate seeing you waste your time like this. It's been six months. You've proven your point. *Enough* already."

"Look at the time," I said, glancing quickly at Dad's watch, which I'd worn every day since he died. "I have to go, Mom. Maybe you should call your perfect son to come over and have tea with you. Sounds like you'd much prefer hearing about his super-exciting life doing *corporate law*."

"You're being dramatic," she said.

I rolled my eyes. "Well, at least I inherited *one* of your traits."

I walked back to my apartment feeling defeated. I was exhausted from work, sure, but the conversation with my mom was almost more tiring. At least at Crawford, clients respected me and saw the value in what I was doing. Mom seemed hell-bent on proving that all the blood, sweat, and tears—three things we had in ample supply at Crawford—were for nothing. *Why does everyone in my life need convincing?* I thought, my mind shifting from my mother to Monica, who still hadn't smiled at me once. *When can I just be myself, and do what I love, and have that be enough?*

FIVE

Deathstyles of the Rich and Famous

*L*ook at this guy," said Monica, rolling her eyes. She was talking—not to me, of course, but just to the general vicinity—about a man in cargo shorts with a camera around his neck, who was now standing in the Crawford foyer. "Some people have no shame."

Yes, there was the man, fanny pack and all, avoiding eye contact with us as he casually strolled around as if he were browsing for furniture. He was far from the first tourist I'd seen in my seven months at Crawford—at least one or two a week popped in, usually trying to discreetly take a photo before slinking back outside onto Madison Avenue. At first I found it super rude (just what grieving people need—a guy with a zoom-lens camera) and super *weird*. Call me boring, but when I jet off somewhere, nothing on my vacation itinerary involves death. In fact, I like death to be left entirely out of the plans. Zero death.

But after months at Crawford, I finally started to understand why tourists—the kind of strange, stalker-ish ones, anyway—were always popping in to check the place out. Crawford was a link to the famous New Yorkers memorialized within its walls—attracting fans of everyone from Judy Garland to Biggie Smalls. Unlike LA, where people can creepily ride around scoping out celebrity homes, New York's elite live high up in the sky in unreachable penthouses protected by doormen and elevator men. Even if you wanted to go all fan girl on Ryan Gosling in his driveway (and come on, wouldn't you feel a little silly?), it's not in the cards. Because there aren't driveways in New York. Just locked-up parking garages where three security guards would spot that fanny pack coming from a mile away.

There has always been an unspoken rule in New York that you don't go up to a celebrity at Per Se or Le Cirque and ask for an autograph or get all weird asking them to take a selfie with you. Maybe it's because some of my friends are famous, or I've spent too many fund-raiser dinners sitting near actual celebrities like Elton John and quasi-celebrities like the Kardashians, but I've always loved this about New Yorkers. We can't be bothered to get all caught up in the hype. Most of the time, I didn't even notice when I was hanging out with someone famous. One night at a club, a cute, taller guy pulled me onto the dance floor—it was only later that I realized it was Vince Vaughn. There was also the time I was sitting next to Pharrell, who was singing along to the song blasting through the speakers. "You have such a great voice," I said, completely oblivious. "You could be a singer!" He just smiled and said he'd think about it.

My casualness around Hollywood types might also have been the reason Tony had called me into his office a week earlier to talk to me about "what the hell I'm doing here," as he put it. After almost a year at Crawford, my title was still "receptionist"—at least officially—but on top of answering phones and greeting clients, I made an effort to get involved with every part of funeral planning. The other receptionists were pretty much there to collect a paycheck. I knew I wasn't there for the money. Though the work was fulfilling, my salary was basically a trip to Europe and a handbag, not exactly lifestyle-altering income.

"What would you think about being a little more involved?" Tony asked.

"I thought I already was!" I said.

"Well, yeah, sure. And you're doing great helping clients plan services. The thing is, I can't do much with the pay and title. Union bullshit. It's just what it is. But you seem like you want to take on more. And, you know, I think you've seen enough. You know how this place works." Tony paused. "You're ready. Do you feel ready?"

I nodded. "Oh, absolutely."

"I figured as much," he said. "I know you have experi-

ence with these . . . people." He said the last word very carefully. "I just can't make it, you know, official. It's more an
understanding between us. But consider yourself promoted,
in my eyes."

"So . . . kinda like unofficial party planner?" I said, smiling. "For the dead?"

Tony shook his head and laughed. "What am I getting
myself into?" he said. "I want you to keep doing what you're
doing, just spend less time at reception and more time with
the clients. You know, meet with them, find out what they
want—that sort of thing. Then make it happen. As for title, I
was thinking more like director of family services. Does that
work for you?"

"It does," I said.

"You're going to need an office," said Tony, rubbing his
temples.

Oh great, I thought. It wasn't that I didn't want an office—a little privacy would be nice—but the receptionists already hated me. This was going to pretty much seal that
coffin.

"You can move your stuff to the office up front," said
Tony. "Just, you know . . . do it quietly. I don't want to deal
with any union bullshit."

Tony had been asking me for weeks to help out with this
funeral and that funeral—each time having to get permission
from the president of the company, who wasn't exactly
thrilled that I was so involved with clients. But Tony recog-

nized the fact that I really *did* understand his clients in a way no one else at Crawford could. Just a day earlier, a man had called who said his last name was Ballantine. "Is that spelled like the sweater or the scotch?" I asked, both of which are pretty expensive brands. To my amusement, the guy paused and then said, "Wait, *who am I talking to?*"

I even kept my cool the day I ran into Richard Gere while I was restocking tissues before a service (Monica was *freaking*). He politely asked me where the restroom was—of course politely; he's Richard Gere, for God's sake—and so I told him. An hour or so later, we ran into each other again. He was all, "How do you like working here? What's your job like?" and I was all, "In case I forget to tell you later, I had a really great time tonight." Of course, that last part was just in my head. What I actually did was smile and explain that the job was fulfilling, and I enjoyed helping people.

If the guy standing in the foyer was a reminder of anything, it was how different—how *cool*—my job was. (When was the last time Richard Gere used your office's bathroom?) But I also felt a little uneasy with Crawford being another destination, like the Empire State Building or Rockefeller Center. This was a place for grieving. In fact, we had an appointment scheduled in ten minutes, and I was getting nervous that Mr. Fanny Pack was going to make them feel uncomfortable. I wondered if the tourist figured that death on the Upper East Side of Manhattan was somehow less painful. It was easy for most of the Crawford staff to judge the diamond-wearing, mink-coat-covered women and their white-haired husbands who came through Crawford's doors, and to think they weren't totally shattered at the loss of a loved one. But they were, and I knew that the only real difference between the Fifth Avenue widows and anyone else is that people worth millions, even *billions*, are used to the best—and they want the same for funerals. Ornate caskets, stupidly expensive decorations, grand exits (if it's your last good-bye, might as well leave in style)—these were all fair game.

Tony handed me a stack of folders and led me to an office down the hall from his. Monica was *fuming* as Tony explained to her that someone else would have to cover the phones, since I was going to be working on services. I had actually never minded answering phones—it was the first point of contact with clients, and that was important—but I was happy to be in a separate room where I wouldn't hear Monica taking jabs at me.

"So what kind of budget am I working with?" I asked Tony as I flipped through the folders. "I'm not seeing a lot of numbers on here."

Tony let out a laugh. "For those clients? There is no budget. Go all out."

Now *this* was the job I was born to do.

TONY WAS EAGER to show me the ropes. I'm not sure if it was because he was happy to be able to push some of his work off on someone else or if he genuinely appreciated having someone on his team who was excited to be there, but either way, he took me under his wing, and we hit the ground running. First, he told me that there were two golden rules when it came to planning a celebrity funeral: never tell the press *anything*, and always put up barricades, because they'll show up anyway. This made sense: If a famous person died in New York City, he or she was probably going to be brought to Crawford. The seasoned reporters and paparazzi knew this, so they camped out and played their odds. It was like a game of who could out-trick the other. When Heath Ledger died, a reporter pretending to be a family member called up in a convincing Australian accent to try to get information about the service. Photographers posing as florists delivering arrangements once crashed the service of a famous dancer. On the flip side, when Jackie Onassis passed away, an embalmer from Crawford discreetly entered her building and prepped her body in her apartment so that the paparazzi would only get shots of her in an elegant casket—not a body bag. Since I had plenty of experience with the paparazzi through my friends, I knew that privacy was essential—especially at a funeral—and appreciated Tony's diligence.

"WE'LL HAVE our work cut out for us today," said Tony, a few weeks into my new job. It was the day of a rock legend's funeral, and the press were already lined up outside even though we hadn't been returning their calls. This was my first funeral where *everyone* was talking about it—even the "Page Six" reporters who were always writing about my famous friends' love lives showed up to report on who was there. I was a nervous wreck; knowing that the press could document any misstep made me want to throw up a little. My family and friends already thought I had gone off the edge taking a job at a funeral home. The last thing I needed was a public fuckup so they could think I was crazy *and* incompetent.

Tony tackled the press fiasco, while my job was to secure the tour bus. The idea was that people who came to say good-bye could also pay respects to the rocker's drums, which we could keep outside in a massive tour bus. I was pretty proud of this idea—it was the perfect personal touch. But parking it on Madison Avenue was a whole other story, and I wanted to show Tony that I could handle even the craziest of tasks. I woke up at five a.m., slipped on one of my black blazers, and groggily walked over to Crawford hours before the neighbors would even start brewing their coffee. I normally didn't wake up so early for a service, but finding parking for a two-seat sports car is hard enough in Manhattan, never mind a bus the size of many New York City apartments. I was the first one there, and instead of going inside to put down my bag and get a cup of coffee, I went right to the stretch of pavement outside Crawford, held my arms out like an overzealous crossing guard, and waited for the bus to arrive. *Please don't let anyone I know drive by*, I thought, thinking about the look on my mother's face if she saw me standing in the street in my Aerosoles. I could practically hear her: *Elizabeth, what are you* doing?! *Elizabeth, your father and I did not spend hundreds of thousands of dollars on your education so you could be a glorified parking attendant! Elizabeth, why can't you be more like your brother? Elizabeth, Elizabeth, Elizabeth* . . . I was relieved when, fifteen minutes later, the massive bus rolled up next to the curb.

After the bus was in place, my second big task of the morning was to finalize the guest list with the star's assistant, who had been working with the musician for almost twice as long as I'd been alive. We'd been going back and forth about the list for twenty-four hours straight, which was a lot of work, but Tony said that was typical for a famous person's funeral. I knew from planning events at my friends' clubs and restaurants that it was always important to check in with a celebrity's publicist or manager and make sure that the highest-profile guests were on a VIP list. (In this case, that included Tony Bennett and Slash.) A VIP list for a funeral might sound straight-up crazy, but when people are used to extra consideration, they expect it *all* the time. Even at a funeral.

Once the list was made and Tony gave me the okay that the room was ready and the flowers had been laid out, it was also my job to enforce it. Reading names off a list doesn't exactly require a degree in neuroscience, but I knew that one flub could create tension at the door, which was the last thing Tony and I needed. Some famous people were easy to spot; nobody had to check the list the day P. Diddy rolled up to pay his respects at a service. But the moguls and socialites and CEOs were harder to sort out. I had heard of more than one incident of some pissed-off egomaniac screaming at a shaking receptionist, which was a bad way to start a hard enough day. Tony trusted me to usher in the right folks and shoo away anyone else.

The one person I could usually count on showing up un- invited was Herbert the Funeral Groupie. He was an older guy who lived in the neighborhood, and I'm not sure if he was lonely or just really liked funerals, but he couldn't get enough of Crawford. He usually tried to sneak past me with- out a word, and occasionally I would feel bad and let him slip by. What can I say? I had a soft spot for people who ap- preciated a good funeral.

Although Herbert didn't make an appearance on this day, by five p.m. most of the invited guests had arrived. One of the nice things about memorial services is that people tend to arrive on time, so I only had to stand outside with a clipboard for an hour. Once the guests had been ushered in- side, I tiptoed into the largest of Crawford's viewing rooms, where the rocker's service was being held, and stood in the back to watch all my planning come to life (no pun in- tended). In a perfect world, I would have convinced Tony Bennett and Slash to start an impromptu jam session near the casket while the crowd passed a joint around the room, saying, "Hell yeah. This one's for you, brother." But instead, a guitar player, bass player, and piano player who'd performed with the star for years kept it classy with a really moving version of "Vaya con Dios (May God Be with You)." I'd worked with them on the musical selection, and I had to say, it turned out beautifully.

After the service, guests boarded the tour bus and rode to a recording studio in Manhattan. While the service itself had been pretty classic, this was my favorite spin on the day—a *moving* memorial. Once at the studio, a stream of rock royalty came in to pay tribute. I couldn't help but think that this rock star was one of the lucky ones—he would live on everywhere from suburban basements to massive stadiums, his voice streaming out from the amplifiers with every stroke of a chord.

"YOU READY for another one?" Tony asked me as we walked back into Crawford. It was almost midnight, and I'd only gotten five hours of sleep in the past three days. Even though every part of me was exhausted, I wanted to show Tony that I was tough enough to handle this business—and also that he hadn't made a mistake in unofficially promoting me. (Although it felt pretty official around Crawford, where all the receptionists were giving me the cold shoulder.)

"Sure," I said, trying not to sound as tired as I felt. "First thing in the morning."

The next day, I started planning the service for Mr. Wheels, an Italian businessman with a soft spot for million-dollar sports cars. He loved them so much, he had bought more than one hundred Lamborghinis over the years and kept them in a massive garage at his mansion outside Manhattan. The place was like something out of *The Godfather*. Along the long driveway, there were marble statues of horses in valiant poses and *three* ornate fountains where little cherubs spit water out of their mouths. And that was before you even got to the garage, where he kept his prize possessions— rows of yellow, red, and black Lamborghinis lined up like horses at the starting gate.

"This guy is one of the top fine-car collectors in the world," said Bill, standing over the body.

I looked down at Mr. Wheels, thinking he looked a bit like Jimmy Buffet, minus the bright Hawaiian shirt. Delirious from working so many hours, I imagined him giving the cars out, Oprah style. "And *you* get a Lamborghini! And *you* get a Lamborghini!"

Bill covered up Mr. Wheels and opened a bag that the family had sent over.

Inside was a black Lamborghini jacket and a gold chain for Mr. Wheels to be buried in. I tried to keep a straight face while Bill ogled the jacket like he was contemplating buying it.

He wrinkled his face up like Robert De Niro. "Man had taste," he said. I couldn't help but laugh.

I left Bill to start working his magic and went upstairs to

meet Mr. Wheels's son, Nico. I knew right away I was going to like this guy—he was well dressed in Zegna and gave off an air that he was here to do business. "Is that your office over there?" he said without a beat, pointing toward one of the side doors.

"It is," I said, and before I could give him my condolences, I was following Nico into my office, where he sat right down in one of two plush chairs.

"Okay, so the service has got to involve Lamborghinis," he said, sitting on the edge of the seat cushion. "My father, he loved his cars more than anything—except his family. He loved his family the most."

I feverishly jotted down notes while Nico rattled off ideas for his dad's memorial. At the end of our meeting, he told me that he trusted me, and then—maybe deciding that he didn't trust me *enough*—asked for my cell phone number. Mr. Wheels's service wouldn't be for a few days, and he wanted to be able to get in touch in case anything came up before then. "I only want to deal with you," he said, looking me dead in the eyes. "I don't like bullshit. You don't do bullshit. I like you." Before he walked out the door, he turned and winked at me. "Don't worry, I won't really call your cell."

My phone rang for the first time at three in the morning. In my experience, when someone calls you any time after midnight and before seven a.m., it's an emergency, and you pick that shit up.

"Hello?" I said. My voice was groggy.

"Why are you picking up?" Nico said.

I rubbed my eyes and looked at the clock. "Why are you calling me?" I wasn't annoyed—actually, I found Nico's quirkiness kind of awesome, and I also remembered what it was like after my dad died and I'd lie awake at night running through every little detail of his service.

"I was thinking about my father's memorial, and there's one thing we've got to do. Promise me you can make it happen . . ."

I went into Crawford the next morning, even though I technically had the day off. There was too much planning to be done for Mr. Wheels's service, and I needed to make sure everything went according to plan. I'd worked with enough event planners over the years to know that you do *not* make an important client a promise and fuck it up—and I wasn't going to let Nico down, not with the memorial taking place the next day. I spent hours in the front office making calls to Mr. Wheels's staff and coordinating Nico's special requests for his dad's service. It was a lot to pull together in such a short period of time, but crazy demands weren't unusual at Crawford—clients were paying for us to go above and beyond. And I did.

By the time Nico showed up at Crawford on the day of his father's service, we'd been texting for days. I'd seen photos of his family, his dad, his childhood. We had a conversation about what it was like to lose your dad—the guy who's your rock is then just up and gone. It wasn't that standard, fake-ish, "I'm so sorry for your loss" talk. In a lot of industries, it's considered a faux pas to get too close to your clients. But the death biz wasn't like that—and it was pretty hard to cross a boundary line with a guy who called you in the middle of the night. Plus I loved every minute of it; nothing made me feel like I was doing a good job more than when clients opened up to me.

I'll never forget the look on Nico's face when he stepped out of his car and saw many of his father's Lamborghinis lining Madison Avenue. I hadn't slept in three days and was basically running on caffeine fumes, but it was totally worth it for that moment. His eyes welled up with tears, and as friends and family walked up the street toward Crawford, they touched the cars delicately, like Mr. Wheels's spirit was revving within their V12 engines.

"You outdid yourself," Nico said when he saw me. He wiped both his eyes and looked out onto the street with a huge smile on his face. It was like the cars, a herd of Italian stallions, had come to pay their respects, too. I gave him a hug and led him inside. There was one more surprise.

Normally, the main attraction at a wake is the guy in the casket. That's the person everyone comes to see—the life of the death party, so to speak. But I had something extra in mind for Mr. Wheels. At the front of the room, I'd arranged to have his $100,000 model Lamborghini brought in from his home and enclosed in a glass case. (I left out that a small piece of paint had chipped off the side of it as the delivery guys carried it in. "This insured?" one of them asked, the blood rushing from his face. I didn't really know but nodded and waved him on in.)

"You can't have a Lamborghini funeral without any cars in the room," I said. Nico put his hand on my shoulder and nodded in approval, unable to speak for the first time since I'd met him. It was a perfect moment.

As the last guests made their way out, Nico approached me and asked if I'd ride along with him in the procession to the cemetery. "But first," he said, "we have to drive by Dad's house." It's Italian tradition to drive the body by the deceased person's home, which I knew from my mother's side of the family. I was honored Nico would ask me to tag along in his limo, and even more excited to see the procession of Lamborghinis driving through Central Park on their way to the Bronx and eventually into the New York suburbs.

"Just tell whoever's driving Dad's cars that they better watch for potholes," said Nico. I grabbed my walkie-talkie and lowered my voice—my attempt at sounding more authoritative—to relay the message to the twenty Crawford employees standing outside in suits and earpieces. "See? No bullshit," said Nico. "Dad woulda liked you."

WHEN I WALKED into Crawford one morning and heard that the adult son of a foreign billionaire had died, I initially assumed from drugs or alcohol. I vaguely knew of him (I'll call him Dr. Feelgood)—he was that old guy at the club, the one dancing on a table at four a.m., an hour when the lights came on and even the young girls in stilettos and sequined dresses were ready to call it a night. Not Dr. Feelgood; he was calling his pilot, telling him to prepare his private plane for takeoff—it was time to continue the party in a new time zone. It didn't seem out of the realm of possibility that he had perhaps partied a little *too* hard. But when I looked at his folder, I saw that he actually had been sick for a while—he just hadn't told anyone.

I was about to go down to the embalming room to see Bill when Tony called me into his office. "I've got one for you," he said.

I walked in and took a seat, hoping that he'd ask me to work on what was *sure* to be a hell of a funeral. I didn't want to flat-out ask, though. Tony seemed to appreciate my connections and knack for dealing with our clientele, but I had the feeling that if I got a little too comfortable, he might become territorial. A few days before, a client (who happened to be a friend of a family friend) called and asked for me by name. Tony didn't explicitly say it, but when I went to fill him in on the case, I could tell by his tone that he was bothered. I didn't want to step on any toes with this family.

"Think you can help me out with this?" he said without looking me in the eye. He must have known the answer was yes; even when I didn't agree with everything Tony did, I was eager to learn from him what I could and never said no to helping out. On some days, my can-do attitude benefited both of us, like Tony was a teacher and I was the top student in his class. Others, there was this tone, like maybe he kind of resented needing my help.

I nodded respectfully. "Of course."

"The family wants this to be . . . over the top. We need to make anything that they want happen, you hear me?"

"Loud and clear," I said.

An hour later, Dr. Feelgood's family was standing in the foyer. I felt a little embarrassed at the garlic smell wafting from the break room downstairs. It was lunchtime, and Bill and some of the guys had ordered from their favorite Italian restaurant. Tony looked a little more nervous than usual and wiped his hand on the back of his jacket before offering it to the two people standing in front of him. "We're so sorry for your loss," he said.

I ignored Monica's gaze as Tony and I walked the family into his office, very conscious that this was going to be a truly elaborate planning session.

The family sat down and I pulled out a notebook to write down their requests. "Did you have anything particular in mind?" I asked. I noticed that Tony hadn't taken out his binder of flower arrangements. This client was beyond lilies, and Tony was going for a bigger sell.

The man and woman spoke to each other in Spanish for a moment and then turned to face me. Then in English, the woman said, "The best of everything."

Tony nodded, and I could practically see the dollar signs in his eyes. "That's what we're here for," he said. Clearly these people had money to burn, but I still felt a little guilty about letting them overspend on a memorial service. Some of the best funerals I had witnessed since working at Crawford weren't necessarily the most expensive, but the ones that had heart—personalized eulogies, a friend who played guitar, mementos from the person's life scattered around the room. Tony's voice broke my train of thought. "Liz, did you get that?"

I looked up, startled. "Oh, um, yes. Can you say it one more time?"

The woman started talking so fast that even though she was speaking English, I could barely make out what she was saying. *Orchards? No, no, that doesn't make sense. Oh, orchids! Wait, how many? Forty* thousand *dollars' worth?* I wrote it down, waiting, *hoping* that Tony would step in and bring them down to earth. Instead, he nodded as they rattled off other demands: They wanted to fly palm trees in to make the space feel more like home. They also wanted five-foot vases and enough candles to light up a city block.

"And what about the casket?" Tony asked.

I felt a knot in my stomach. I knew what was coming next.

"Oh," said the woman, looking at the man and shrugging. "The best you have."

Tony tried to hide a small smile. "Well, we have a

bronze one. It's a beauty. Top of the line. Bronze through and through, velvet lined . . . you can't do better than that."

"Yes," the woman said. "Fine."

I remembered that casket from when Tony walked me through the options for my dad, and I had practically choked on my horror when he mentioned the price. But he had quickly switched gears when I told him that my dad's office had been all mahogany. "Well then, he should have a mahogany casket," said Tony. Once Tony knew that it made sense for my dad, he didn't push. Spending a lot on a casket seemed crazy to me, especially for cremations, when the whole casket (with the body inside, of course) was burned in the incinerator. I had once asked Bill if Tony ever swapped out the pricey casket, cleaned it up, and put it back in the showroom—the families would never have known—but he swore it never happened. Bill said that Haitians sometimes throw stones on top of the casket after a funeral to crack it a bit, so that the funeral home can't try to resell it, trivia I never got the chance to bring up at a party. As I took down the note for a bronze casket for Dr. Feelgood, I wondered if Tony really just thought that people who could afford the best should have exactly that—or if it was all about the money to him.

After the meeting, I called every prop shop in the city looking for extra ways to turn our chapel into a space suitable for the party boy of honor. Within hours, a crew of twenty people was hanging ornate drapery along the walls, and huge ceramic planters were placed around the room for the palm trees. Then it was time to make the guest list— European royalty would be there, as well as A-list designers, famous musicians, and a whole stream of socialites, some of whom I'd met before, and others flying in from across the globe.

Two days later, the palm trees were in place and our chapel looked more like Bungalow 8, which was, at the time anyway, the chicest hangout in the city. Total bill? $150,000. I tried to keep a straight face as I watched Bill give a few last-minute touches to Dr. Feelgood's body. The family had requested that their brother be buried in his favorite outfit: a Snoopy T-shirt and a pair of neon-green sneakers. They also wanted him to be clutching a bottle of his favorite drink, which is where absinthe came in. I watched Bill delicately place the dead hands around the bottle. The funeral lived up to the hype—hundreds of people came, arriving in their Bentleys and Rolls-Royces. One woman even brought her white Maltese, and even though pets aren't allowed in Crawford, Tony let a few things slide for a six-figure funeral. (She didn't bother to have it on a leash, just walked in and let her four-legged friend mingle with the guests.) But I couldn't shake the feeling that for as many people as there were in attendance—and the place was packed—it all felt a little empty. My fears were confirmed when I saw guests coming out of the bathroom with red noses. Suddenly it made sense why the family had asked if the upstairs bathroom had marble countertops.

I was glad that we could accommodate Dr. Feelgood, a lover of women and booze and who knows what else, with a send-off that felt like *him*. But I thought about my friends— the ones getting a little too old for the club scene, the ones snorting coke at work to keep up with the Wall Street crowd—and I felt relieved that my life didn't revolve around partying anymore. It was one thing to live up your youth at a club, drink in hand. It was another to die that way with gray hair, people getting high before the eulogy starts.

I hated to say it, but it also made me think of my lifelong friend Ben: he had a habit of going out and going out *hard*. Besides Gaby and me, his best friends were trust-fund babies, club owners, or trust-fund-baby club owners. There was always a lot of music, a lot of booze, and a lot of money being thrown around. It scared me a little to see someone who had so much potential to make a difference in the world just party it all away. I'd gone through a party phase of my own, but I'd grown out of it. In some ways, my dad's illness helped me mature faster than many of my friends. I knew that life wasn't just about crazy get-togethers and dancing until the sun came up, that it could end any moment, even when you least expected it.

At the end of the service, after the last of the guests had gotten back into the same fancy cars that had brought them in the first place, I walked into the now-empty room that had been filled with the sounds of people kissing each other on both cheeks and telling stories about the guy in the casket. Now it was just the two of us among a sea of wilting orchids. "Wherever you are, I hope you're having a good time," I whispered. Then I picked up a large arrangement—it was almost as big as me—and carried it out of the room, down the stairs, and into the back of a town car that was taking me home. I thought I'd invite a few friends over for a little dinner party and arrange the flowers all over the table.

Instead I went home and fell asleep, alone next to a four-foot tower of orchids.

THE HARDEST high-profile funeral, though, was the one I didn't see coming. I could tell from the giddy expression on Monica's face that someone major was behind closed doors with Tony when I walked in for my shift, but I had no idea how personal it would become. On this particular day, it was obvious by the heightened energy that whoever had come in was beyond just famous—Monica even said hello to me in all her excitement. But she wasn't the one I was worried about. After seeing Tony handle clients, I cringed with compassion thinking about whomever he was up-selling in his office.

A few minutes later, I followed my inkling upstairs, where Tony was standing over a fancy coffin with a velvet interior. My eyes darted from him to a very famous actor and his brother. We had been at a few parties together over the years, but we'd never really talked other than your basic "Nice to meet you's" among the *thud-thud-thud* of club music. The awkward thing about working at a funeral home was that it was never really necessary to ask, "What brings you here?" The more accurate and uncomfortable question was, "Who?"

"Mike?" I said, not sure where to begin. "What . . . I mean . . . who . . . I'm so sorry." I was just about to reintroduce myself, not convinced the recognition would be mutual, when he interrupted my thought.

"Liz, right?" he asked, coming toward me. He looked relieved, more relieved than you'd expect for someone bumping into someone he'd shared little more than a bottle of Ketel One with. "What are you . . . do you *work* here?"

I smiled. "I do. Let me help you."

Tony gave me a look like, *You got this?* and I nodded. It's not like we worked on commission—my assisting meant he could take a breather before the next client came in. Still, he didn't leave the room entirely, instead shifting over to the corner so that he could supervise what I was doing, and probably so he could jump in if I royally messed up.

"May I ask who we're looking for?" I said, placing my hand on the outside of the mahogany casket that Mike was staring at intently.

Without moving his eyes, Mike whispered, "My sister." His voice quivered and he looked down. "She was killed in a motorcycle accident yesterday."

I placed my hand on his arm and steered him and his

brother toward the other side of the room. He said his sister had been in her twenties. She didn't need to be buried in a stuffy wood coffin with a red interior. We stopped in front of a shiny white casket.

"How about this one?" I said. I knew Tony would give me an earful later—the white casket was almost half the price of some of the others—but it would be perfect for Mike's sister. From the way Mike made it sound, she had been a dynamic girl with a casual sense of style. Her memorial should reflect that.

Mike and his brother gave it the once-over, then nodded in agreement.

"Okay, then," I said, keeping my voice soft and guiding them out of the room—while viewing urns and caskets was a necessary step in planning any funeral, I never liked to let clients linger in there too long. It was the saddest of the rooms, to me, because unlike the memorial rooms, where wakes were held and families shared stories about the person who had passed, this room was just logistics. The body had to go *somewhere*, and these were the options.

I showed Mike the room where his sister's service would be held. He looked exhausted, his eyes swollen and sagging, but he tried to take it all in. "Where will she go?" he asked, staring at the carpet. I pointed toward the front of the room. He just stood there, and the weight of his sadness filled the whole space. It was like his heart was beating through the speakers, slowly, mournfully. I had to do something.

"What did your sister like to do for fun?" I said, breaking the rhythm.

Mike didn't hesitate. "Horses. She *loved* horses. When we were kids, we had to sit through her equestrian competitions and they were like hours long . . ."

His thought drifted off somewhere I couldn't follow— he was in his memories, with her. I knew the feeling. Sometimes, after my father died, I'd talk to him without even realizing I was doing it, like we had entered some bubble that all the other living people and all the other dead people couldn't get into. Sometimes I even called his phone without thinking about it. I was devastated when my cell phone had died, the last voice mail I'd had from him gone for good. I felt a similar pang when, eight months after Dad died, my mom had finally changed her outgoing message at home to say, "You've reached Francesca." Not "Brett and Francesca," like they had always had.

"Do you want to bring in some of her riding things?" I said. "And maybe some photos of her? I can arrange everything—just put it all in a box and leave it with me, and I'll set it up myself."

"You'd do that?" Mike said. The relieved look came over his face again. This time, he even smiled. "That would be great. My mom would love it, too. That would be really nice."

I stayed late that night waiting for the box to arrive. I figured an assistant would bring it over, but Mike walked it in himself—he said he needed to make sure it all got there safely. I took the box and gave him a hug, then went to work setting up his sister's things. A well-loved black riding jacket, the buttons coming loose at the seams. A framed photo of her in riding gear. Blue ribbons from competitions she'd won years earlier. It could have been the contents of any girl's room. I placed the photos around her coffin next to white candles. Then I tucked her ribbons into the side of the casket. There were other belongings, too, that I displayed around the room—books she loved, her favorite sweatshirt. Things people would remember her by. Things people would look at and say, "Remember the time she . . ." I still wasn't totally used to being alone in a room with a dead body, but I couldn't avoid looking at her—Bill had covered all the bruises from the accident, and you'd never have known how she'd died. It felt surreal that this girl, almost my age, was herself a thing of the past—her belongings now like artifacts in a museum.

When Mike and his family arrived the next morning, I greeted them at the door. His mom paused and took a deep breath before entering the building, and then I guided them to the steps. Families were always allowed some private time with their loved one before other guests were allowed up. "You're coming too, aren't you?" said Mike, motioning toward the stairs. I hadn't been planning on it—I wouldn't have wanted to intrude on such a personal moment—but I didn't want to turn down the invitation either.

Mike's mom threw her arms around me when I got to the top of the stairs. "Honey, thank you," she said, crying. I handed her a Kleenex, which I always kept on me, just in case. Mike's brother was already at the front of the room looking at the photos.

"It's like you re-created her bedroom," said Mike. "I can feel her in here." He took a moment to fight back tears. "It's so her."

In that moment, I thought about all the other times Mike and I had bumped into each other since we were teenagers. Drunk nights dancing. Our friends throwing down thousands of dollars on drinks at a corner table. We never talked about anything real. We certainly never talked about family—or death. The life that so many of my friends were still living seemed more superficial by the day. On the rare occasion I went out, I couldn't help but feel like all the things that had once felt so fun were a little bit . . . silly.

When it was all over, I was completely drained; there weren't enough cappuccinos in all of Manhattan to revive me. I grabbed my bag and started walking home, thinking about Mike and what life would be like for his family now. That's one of the funny things about funerals: when it's all said and done, most people dry their tears and go about their lives. But when it's a person you really loved, the loss stays with you . . . and in a lot of ways, feels even worse after the service. I thought about my dad and how there had been a line out the door of people waiting to pay their respects to him. I kissed them and hugged them and thanked them for coming. But that night, I was all alone. The party was over. My dad was gone. I wasn't getting him back. I hated that Mike was now going to have to go through that.

Just as I felt my eyes well up, I saw two familiar figures coming toward me. First I made out my mother's face, then my brother's. I barely had enough energy to drag myself back to my apartment, much less deal with whatever unsolicited opinion my mom was inevitably going to share. But it was too late—she had spotted me. There was no turning around.

I knew how I looked: My hair, which I had blown dry that morning, was now plastered against my head in a messy ponytail. My eyeliner was smudged below my eyes from tearing up when, during the service, Mike read a note he wrote for his sister. My ugly black blazer was wrinkled from spending two hours at my desk looking over folders for services taking place the next day. *Please don't say anything*, I thought. *Please just let this slide.*

Mom's eyes stopped on my shoes, and I swear, she let out a gasp—like a rat had run across my feet.

"I . . . it's . . . it's not a good time," I said, holding my hand out, as if it would keep her words away. "I'm really tired."

"Elizabeth," Mom said, looking like she might actually faint, right there on the pavement. Then, in a hushed voice:

"What are you *wearing?*" She said it less like a question and more like an accusation.

I didn't have the energy. There was just nothing left in my tank. A full day of death had sucked the life out of me.

"They're called Aerosoles, Mom," I said, walking past her. "And they're comfortable as hell."

SIX

What a Mob Scene

$\mathcal{C}$rawford had arranged its fair share of mob funerals over the years. I guess it made sense: New York City had been home to the five well-known mob families for decades—and that was just the Italian mob. The Five Families, as they're called, date back to the 1930s. And while it seemed that things had gotten less violent over the years, Bill remembered a story about a funeral home in the outer boroughs owned by a mobster, which was, of course, where lots of Mafia types held services for loved ones. During one funeral, the family was shouldering the casket down the stairs when a rival family walked up and gunned one of the pallbearers down. He slumped to the ground and rolled down the stairs, and everyone else dropped the casket and ran inside the second they heard the gunshot. There was also the story of the Jewish banker who had gotten wrapped up with mobsters back in the sixties and worked for "the family" for years, helping them squeeze dirty money out of business deals and God knows what else. The service was going along as usual—people had paid their respects, the rabbi was giving a blessing and talking about what a loss the whole thing was—when the dead guy's son couldn't take it anymore. "My dad was *not* a good man!" he said, jumping up from his seat. "He was a criminal who ran Chicago for Al Capone! This funeral is *over!*" And, you know, so it was.

And then there was the time when I saw a six-foot-five Russian man who had been beaten to death brought in. "Had to be a mob job," said Bill, looking down at the man's bruised face. "I've never seen someone killed like this. Just pure hate." The weirdest part was the way the body was delivered: two guys drove it from Brooklyn themselves and then waited outside while Bill did the embalming. They just waited there, for hours. Afterward, when Bill was done, they took the body right back and drove away. "*Definitely* a mob job," said Bill, walking back to the prep room.

But my first mob funeral started with a phone call. Nothing unusual, just some guy saying that his relative Sophia had prearranged her funeral with us—it was actually totally normal for people to come in and preplan (and prepay for) their own service—and that she was dead. Things only got weird when he started talking about Sophia's son, Sal. Sal was in a high-security prison, and the family hoped that he would be able to make it to Sophia's funeral. She would have wanted that.

"Oh, okay," I said, not quite sure what he wanted me to do about it. If you wanted bagpipers or flowers from halfway around the world, I was your girl. Prison release wasn't part of my repertoire. "I'll see what I can do."

Sure enough, the number for the warden at the high-security prison was listed on Sophia's prearrangement forms. Whatever Sal had done, Sophia still wanted him to come say good-bye, and I wanted to make that happen. Calling prisons wasn't really part of my job, but helping people get through the first few stages of grieving was. I couldn't imagine not having been able to see my dad one last time.

After hours of back-and-forth calls with the warden, he finally let me talk to Sal. Right away, I noticed his Queens accent—or more specifically, his *Italian* Queens accent. He sounded just like some family members on my mom's side, many of whom still lived across the river from Manhattan. Many of my friends had never been to Queens; it was yet to become a trendy destination for foodies. One time, in high school, I invited a couple of my prep school friends to dinner at my Italian grandma's house. During the ride over, we drove by a series of attached houses—the old-school ones made of red brick, where one family lives on the top floor and another on the bottom. On seeing all the homes with two doors, my friend Ben said, "Look at that, they have separate entrances for their staff."

I secretly felt a little bad for my friend—he didn't know what he was missing. I adore the Italian side of my family. The pasta, the cheese, the way it takes twenty minutes to say hello and good-bye to everybody and then just as you're almost out the door, someone pulls the cannoli platter out of the fridge and you're taking off your coat again. I love it all.

So the phone call. I let Sal know the basics: The service would take place in two days. A priest would be there. Yes, there would be security. No, I did not have a guest list, not yet, but I would contact another family member. Sal told me that he hoped he could make it—it was all up to the warden. "I hope so too," I told him.

That night, I went home and did some Googling to see if I could find out more about Sophia. While there wasn't so much about *her*, I found link after link about her husband, who had been a mob boss before he was killed a decade before, presumably by a hit man. Sal took over the family business, and *he* ended up in jail after killing an unarmed guy in what might have been an inside job.

"Do you think Sal will be at the funeral?" I asked Bill.

He shook his head. "From high-security prison? No way."

"I guess prison officials don't cry tears of sympathy when a murderer loses someone *he* loves," I said.

By the morning of the funeral, I hadn't heard a word from the prison about whether or not Sal would be able to attend, but I couldn't stop thinking about it. Bill had done an amazing job making Sophia look less like an eighty-year-old dead woman and more like an older, sassy movie star with great taste in lipstick, and I busied myself arranging red roses—Sophia's request—around the viewing room. The family had no other requests, which also meant there was nothing left in the budget for me to work with, but I hated how bare the room looked. I ran down the hall to a storage room where we kept random supplies like tissues and lighters, and grabbed as many candles and glass vases as I could find. I scattered them around the viewing room and dimmed the lights. Sophia may have been the wife of a mobster and the mother of a mur-derer, but I still wanted her to have a nice funeral. There was something so lonely about a casket in an empty room. What kind of life did you live if nobody shows up to your funeral?

Bill and I stood around for the next hour and a half, waiting for guests to appear. Just as I was starting to get ner-vous, two men in dark suits walked into the foyer.

"Anybody here yet?" they asked.

"Are you friends of Sophia's?" I asked.

"Uh, yeah," said one of the guys. "We'll be standing at the door. Nobody's here yet, right?"

"That's correct," I said.

I watched as he made a few phone calls, and then within minutes, five black town cars pulled up in front of the build-ing. Out walked the priest, a group of men in black suits and black ties, and several women, some with diamond earrings that were so big they looked like they might rip right through their earlobes.

"I'm sorry for your loss," I said, shaking the hand of one of the men. Nobody had introduced himself, and it was hard to tell who, exactly, was in charge. Did Sal have any brothers or sisters? Were these friends? Family? Whoever they were, and whatever "business" they were in, I wanted them to feel welcome. Sophia deserved that.

More and more guests filed in, and I escorted them into the viewing room. That's where I saw a man who looked in his midforties standing near the casket. He was wearing a pin-striped suit, and for a second, I thought it was Sal saying good-bye to his mom. I don't know if he was really guilty of murder or not—okay, probably, he was *probably* guilty—but a part of me ached for this family. When Sophia's husband died, what did people say? I thought of my mom, and the hundreds of people who had lined up to shake her hand and hug her at Dad's wake. They all had such wonderful things to say about the man she loved. Did Sophia ever have that? And who would be there to hear those wonderful things about *her* if Sal didn't show?

After another minute or so, the man in the pinstripes sat down in the back. Nobody was talking to him, and I realized there was no way it was Sal—too many people would have been hugging him otherwise. For the next hour, I shifted my gaze from the clock to the front door, desperately wishing that Sal would walk through.

He never did. I pictured him sitting alone in a cell, griev-ing for his mother and feeling like he had failed her in some way. I wondered what their last conversation had been—the words they had said, if they had any idea that it would be the final time they spoke. The whole point of a funeral was to bring people together, not just to honor the dead, but to help one another grieve. I may have holed up in a room after my dad died, but that was my choice; there was an entire apartment filled with people to comfort me if I had wanted. Sal was alone. Sophia was dead. And I couldn't help but think that there was something very unfinished about the whole thing.

MY BIG CONTAINER of Fage yogurt was missing. I know, not exactly a code red, but I had written my name on it with black Sharpie and there was nobody else at Crawford named Elizabeth. (Nor anyone who ate Greek yogurt, for that matter.) And the week before, my kale and adzuki bean soup had gone missing. My name was on that, too. I suspected Monica, but it was hard to tell. Two of the other receptionists had also been icing me out, and I couldn't tell if I was getting paranoid that everyone was talking about me or if I was being terrorized by lunch thieves.

I took the Sharpie out and taped a note to the fridge: *If you took my yogurt, please put it back. Thanks. —Elizabeth*

Just as I was about to ask Monica directly—I was starving, and I didn't have time to walk over to Lexington Avenue to pick up a sandwich—Tony tapped me on the shoulder, snapping me out of my thoughts.

"You think you could come into my office for a second?" he said, beet red.

"Of course! Can it wait a couple of minutes, though? I'm trying to figure out what happened to my lunch and—"

"It can't wait a minute. Just come in and sit there, please," he said.

When I walked in, I saw two women sitting on armchairs across from a couch. The one who looked like she was in her late forties was wearing a short, tight dress that looked two sizes too small. The other, who was probably in her early twenties, was wearing a tight black dress with spaghetti straps and no bra. I was afraid her boobs were actually going to pop out, tearing her spaghetti straps and flinging them right into Tony's eyes. They both had crinkly hair that seemed like it may have been teased a few too many times; long, squared-off fingernails with French manicures; and an overload of what I thought must be cubic zirconia. Nobody in their right mind would walk out of their house wearing that much bling without a security detail.

Tony motioned for me to take a seat next to him on the couch.

"Pleased to meet both of you," I said, wishing I'd at least had the chance to read their folder before coming into the meeting. I never met with families unprepared. Who were these women? Who died? And who, for the love of God, told them that five-inch, patent-leather platform heels were in fashion?

Just as I went to sit down, the older of the women hopped up from her seat and plopped down next to Tony. He gave me a look that said, *Help me*, but I didn't know what to do other than squeeze between them (holy awkward). So I gave Tony my best *I'm sorry* face and sat down in the chair. It was still warm and a little sweaty. (I guess that's what happens when your skirt rides halfway up your ass in a leather chair.) But I just smiled and waited to see what would happen next.

"We want a harpist to play," said the older woman, looking only at Tony. She was sitting closer to him now, to the point where their legs were touching on the sofa. *Is she hitting on him?* I thought. *No, impossible.* Tony was a nice enough guy, and he had taught me a lot, but he wasn't exactly Ryan Gosling.

Tony, red in the face, quickly explained that Crawford had a harp on the premises, and a harpist that we used regularly. (When you host funerals every day, it helps to have a team of musicians, florists, and caterers on call.) Rather than spending extra time pushing them toward a string quartet or a team of bagpipers as he normally did, he just said he would be happy to arrange their requests. The woman nudged even closer to him, and Tony looked at me, panicked, as if to say, *Get me out of here.*

"Make sure the strings are really *tight*," said the woman, overemphasizing the last word.

This can't be happening. This isn't happening.

She leaned forward again, this time so that her left boob was practically grazing Tony's lapel. I felt bad that Tony was in such an uncomfortable situation, but it was also kind of hilarious. I couldn't figure out what this woman was trying to get at with the whole I'll-show-you-mine routine. Some customers tried to negotiate prices, but she had yet to ask for a discount. (I'm pretty sure Tony—a happily married man, by the way—would have given her a deal just to have an excuse to get off that couch.)

"Liz, maybe you have some suggestions for these ladies?" said Tony. I was trying so hard to keep a straight face, I knew if I looked him in the eye I would crack. It was clear now that he hadn't brought me in to help plan the funeral—he just wanted a witness so that he wasn't accused of sexual harassment or whatever else they were trying to pull. Tony was smart enough to know that two scantily clad women *probably* weren't throwing their panties in his face for no reason.

I suggested a few different floral arrangements, as well as some musical selections for the harpist—nothing out of the ordinary. Then, sensing that Tony was about to jump out the window, I helped to tally up their total for them to let them know the damage. If I had talked to Tony beforehand and knew the 411 on the client, I perhaps wouldn't have almost fallen off my chair when the two women picked up their oversized purses and pulled out $30,000 in cash.

I looked at Tony and raised my eyebrows. *Are these*

women seriously trying to hand over stacks of $100 bills?
What kind of crazy person walks the streets of New York City
with that much cash on them? I'd seen women get their
purses stolen on the subway. It happened fast: usually the
woman was sitting on the blue plastic seat with her bag on
her lap, and right as the automated announcement "Please
stand clear of the closing doors" blared through the car,
some guy scooped up her handbag and ran up the stairs and
through the turnstiles. Done. Gone. Arrivederci, dahling.

Instead of suggesting that maybe, *maybe* they pay with a
credit card or something less shady than wads of sweaty
cash, Tony accepted their money and quickly wrote up a re-
ceipt. He went from looking like a scared virgin about to get
his first lap dance to a smooth-talking businessman in two
seconds flat. After the women left, I asked Tony who the hell
they were—and where they got that kind of money. He al-
luded to the fact that they might be mob-related, although
there was no way to know for sure. Not that it mattered,
anyway—paying in cash might have seemed shady, but it was
hardly illegal.

The whole scene got me thinking about the difference
between good business and dirty business—and everything
in between. These women—and their mobster husbands—
might have been skirting the law in one way or another, but
they certainly weren't the only ones.

I was at Crawford when Bernie Madoff was arrested for
losing billions of dollars of his investors' money in a Ponzi

scheme. The I-bankers and traders, though they weren't breaking the law, weren't exactly keeping it clean either. New York was money hungry, and even guys like Tony weren't immune to it. I wasn't naïve enough to think that he'd refuse the women's business; money talks, and in Manhattan, it screams. But he didn't even hesitate when they pushed the bills into his palm. Tony was no Bernie, but he was willing to cash in and not ask questions. But I suppose I didn't ask any either.

SEVEN

Holy Shit

$\mathcal{I}$ see ghosts.

It sounds crazy. I know. But the truth is, my mom and I have always had "visitors," and we've never been much bothered by them—in fact, they can be quite comforting. My mom's father died when she was a girl, leaving her without a dad for most of her life. Except she always saw him . . . in her closet. Not in a scary way or anything, just kind of standing there, making sure she was okay. When my parents moved into their Upper East Side apartment and Mom told Dad that her father was hanging out in the closet at night, he thought she was nuts. I was only a few years old at the time, and they never mentioned any of this to me. Then one morning after I had crawled into their bed, I looked at both of them and casually asked, "Who is the man who lives in your closet?"

Dad was officially spooked after that.

The weird thing was, I never saw ghosts at Crawford. I only felt them—and I wasn't the only one.

After the promotion, Monica had stopped talking to me altogether—so I was surprised the day she came running out of the bathroom, and, seeing as I was the only one around, grabbed my arm. "You have to see this," she said, pulling me down the hall with her. Bill had told me that Crawford was haunted—presumably by the wife of Mr. Crawford, although with all the dead bodies going in and out, it was hard to say. I didn't believe it at first—ghosts didn't usually hide themselves around me—but during my late-night shifts, I *did* notice that the lights would inexplicably flicker, and the blinds would go from up to down, or vice versa. You know, little stuff that makes you scratch your head and gives you goose bumps but doesn't necessarily convince you that Casper is going to pop out from behind the curtains.

When Monica and I got upstairs, we saw the doorknob to the bathroom turn, and then the door closed. "Did you see that shit?" she said, her eyes wide. She was actually clutching on to my arm, which might have been our first point of physical contact, well . . . ever.

I nodded. "Should we check it out?"

Monica stood behind me as we inched our way toward the bathroom. My heart raced as I turned the knob, and I felt a chill run up my back as I opened the door to reveal an empty bathroom. Something about the room felt sad and cold. I thought of a story that Bill had told me, about a man who had killed himself in that bathroom. It had happened years before. The man had come in to plan his wife's funeral and said that he'd like to prearrange the same exact service for himself—right down to the last detail—for when the time came. Tony was apparently happy to make a double sale, and even though it sounds pretty morbid, it wasn't that unusual. After the man signed on the dotted line and handed over the payment, he politely excused himself to the restroom, where he *shot himself in the head*. Just like that. Tony called the police—what else can you do?—and called the family. When they got to his apartment, they found that the man had laid out a suit that he wanted to be buried in. With his wife gone, he just didn't want to be here anymore. He wanted to be with her. Although maybe, he also wanted to be in the Crawford bathroom, where Monica and I stood, trying not to girl-scream at the turning knob.

The harder part was in the *not* seeing. When I paused talking to my mom in the kitchen of our country house once, she just shrugged and said, "You saw that, too?" referring to a ghost outside of the window. Neither of us was scared. Same goes for when I moved into my own apartment, only to find the ghost of a guy I had never met sitting on my bed, feet hanging over the edge, looking at the wall. It was just that one time—I never saw him again. Although I always wondered why he had stayed in the first place and if he'd ever come back.

I always hoped a little that my dad would come back to me, Mom, and Max, and he did. Except he was much less obvious about the whole thing. Max swears that Dad continues to steal his tuxedo studs as an ongoing joke. Once, while getting ready for a wedding, Max searched his whole room up and down and couldn't find them, even though he always kept them in a box, in a safe. He had just worn them to an event the week before and was meticulous about putting them away. He called me and my mom in hysterics: "Dad gave them to me," he said, crying. "I wouldn't lose them. I *know* I put them away."

My mom felt bad for him and said she would search her apartment—although it was really just a gesture to make Max feel better. When she opened her closet door, her eyes went toward a handbag on the shelf . . . and, I swear to God or whoever else might be listening, the studs were on top. Mom hadn't seen Max in a month. There was no possible way the studs could have made their way onto her purse. And yet, there they were.

I had had a similar experience in Italy. After a week of traveling alone, I was in a cab on my way to the airport in Milan when I realized that a gold pin my father had given me—and that I brought everywhere—wasn't in the velvet jewelry pouch along with my diamond earrings. I knew I had put the pin in there the night before, and I had triple-checked that morning. I was beside myself and struggled with my basically nonexistent Italian telling the driver he had to turn around and go back to the hotel. They hadn't cleaned my room yet—it was only five a.m.—so I was allowed back upstairs to ransack the room, turning over every cushion and every pillow. Nothing. After sobbing the whole forty-five-minute drive *back* to the airport, I dug into my bag to get my sunglasses to cover my red, puffy eyes. And that's when I saw it: the pin, resting right on the "nose" of the sunglasses case, staring right back at me. I was relieved, but then it hit me: The weather in Milan had been cold, gray, and rainy the whole time I was there. I never once had put my sunglasses on. I threw my hands in the air and looked up. "Are you *trying* to give me a heart attack?" I said. Then, I grabbed my suitcase and headed toward the terminal.

What I'm saying is: my dad was very much still with me after he died. I could feel him—and I still do. But does that mean there's a heaven? I don't know. Unlike most of the staff members at Crawford, who were *very* Catholic, I'd always considered myself more of a spiritual person . . . but not necessarily religious. Gaby and Ben liked to push me into deep conversations about what happens after we die, and while I tried not to think too much about an afterlife (wasn't the whole point to live *this* life to the fullest instead of hedging our bets on some never-never land?), I believed my father was somewhere.

"Well, scientifically, he has to be," said Ben one day, eating Twizzlers on my couch.

"What do you mean, 'scientifically'?" I asked.

"Conservation of energy," he said. "Einstein. Energy cannot be created nor destroyed; therefore, there needs to be some sort of afterlife. Otherwise, where does someone's energy go when they die?"

Ben's logical explanation brought me a lot more comfort than any religion. I may have studied different faiths at the Gallatin School at NYU—I even minored in the study of the Quran—but it all seemed more cultural to me than spiritual. My professors and I talked about death on an academic level; it wasn't about *my* beliefs, but rather, other people's philosophies. Knowing so much about how different cultures view death definitely made "the end" less intimidating, but it also made it less emotional. Look, I sure hope there's a higher power. But I'm just not convinced. Blame it on the watered-down version of Catholicism I was raised with, or maybe I'm just another skeptic. New York City seems to be filled with those.

I MAY NOT have been the most amazing Catholic, but when Tony called a staff meeting to announce that a cardinal would be having his wake at Crawford before a procession to St. Patrick's Cathedral for the funeral, even I got a little excited. I was *technically* part of the church. My mom had made sure Max and I were baptized, and she made us go to Sunday school (which was actually on Tuesdays) so that we could get the other sacraments. I was a bit of a disaster:

When I was five, the Sunday school teacher gave me a coloring book displaying heaven and hell. (Kind of intense for a bunch of kindergartners, but I digress.) I asked her what heaven was, and she said, "Where all happy things are, and everyone you love. But only good Catholics go to heaven."

"What about Jewish people?" I said, thinking of my dad.

She paused for a minute, let out a deep sigh, and said, "No. They don't get in."

I proceeded to cry until my mom picked me up.

Anyway, the cardinal. Crawford was buzzing with energy, with calls coming in from the Vatican (yes, the freaking Vatican) with instructions. Even though I wasn't religious, I hoped to earn some points with whatever God might be watching by making sure the wake went off without a hitch. Plus, Tony was about to lose his mind. He was Catholic— and just about the last thing he wanted to do was screw up the funeral of someone a lot closer to the Big Guy than him.

"Liz, there's a package coming in from the Vatican," Tony told me. "You need to keep an eye out for it. We need to make sure every single thing is taken care of."

We handled personal items for people all the time, so I didn't see what the big difference was. But I gave Tony a serious nod—this was no time for joking around—and listened to the messages to make sure I had everything correct. "I wonder who else from the church will be here," I said to Monica, who was already back to hating me after our short-lived ghost bonding session.

"I thought you were Jewish," she said flatly, before going to find one of the other receptionists.

When the package finally arrived—it was more like a giant case—I couldn't wait to see what was inside. The first thing we pulled out was a golden scepter, like the thing Ariel's father waves around in *The Little Mermaid*. (I may or may not have hummed "Under the Sea" while setting everything up.) There was also a white robe and an ornate hat that looked a lot like a crown.

I spent most of that afternoon in the embalming room with Bill. He had received specific instructions about how to prep the body and dress it, and while that was normal—especially for religious services—there was something about this that felt even more sacred. This particular cardinal had meant a lot to New York City: On September 11, then-mayor Rudy Giuliani had summoned him to drive downtown to help with a disaster. According to reports, the cardinal—who was, at the time, the archbishop of New York—had no idea what was happening in lower Manhattan. Not, at least, until he found himself standing in a church near Wall Street, where he waited, painfully, for the bodies to be brought in. He spent days down there, anointing the dead and giving out rosaries, sometimes wearing a gas mask so that he could breathe with all the dust and debris. Uptown, I was in a classroom with a bunch of other eleventh graders, many of whom had parents or older siblings who worked near or in the towers. A bunch of us had just gotten back to school from getting bagels when a girl in my class came in and, sounding confused, said, "A plane just flew into a building or something." My first thought was small plane, small building—an unfortunate accident in a different borough. Then we all were called to an assembly, where the dean of the school, Mr. Allen, broke the news and offered to let students use the school's landlines, since nobody was getting cell service. He was a friend of my family, and so he scooted me into his office so I could dial my mom, first thing. Before I could get a word in, Mom said, "Put Mr. Allen on the phone." She told him that she was coming to get me, and as many other kids from the neighborhood as would fit in her car. Even though the school was just a mile across town from our apartment, it took two hours to get home because the cops had shut down Central Park, blocking off key roads to get across. We huddled up with Max's buddies, desperately waiting for calls from friends and family who worked in the World Trade Center to come in. A few never did.

After the attacks, the cardinal led funerals—many of which were for policemen and firefighters who had died trying to rescue others. He even consoled former New York City mayor Ed Koch, who was Jewish. As the story goes, the cardinal saw Koch crying at St. Patrick's Cathedral on Fifth Avenue. When he asked why he was crying, Koch allegedly told him that he'd heard that a fire department chaplain had been killed—one of the people he knew from being in office.

The cardinal was happy to finally share some *good* news: The chaplain had actually survived. He was okay. One small moment of joy in an otherwise tragic day. "Here was a Jewish former mayor crying over a monsignor after having lit a candle at St. Patrick's Cathedral. Where but in New York?" the cardinal later told the Associated Press.

Bill spent hours stressing over every detail with the cardinal's body. Upstairs, Tony was busy getting the casket in order. The Vatican had very specific rules about that, too. The casket, which had to be special-ordered, had to be lined with red velvet. I helped Tony double-check the order, since each rank in the Catholic Church has its own casket requirements, and we *both* wanted to make sure that we got it right.

I was surprised when the cardinal's casket was brought into one of the smaller viewing rooms on the fourth floor. The newspapers had already written about the cardinal's death—surely there would be crowds. But as it turned out, only a few select members of the clergy were allowed to view the body. Everyone else was waiting at St. Patrick's Cathedral, where the funeral was taking place. I watched as the clergy members covered the casket in a special white cloth called a "pall" with a big cross on it, and then as it was loaded into a hearse. At the cathedral, more than 750 mourners, plus 150 church dignitaries, said good-bye to the cardinal. The whole place was lit up with incense and candles, and the next day, the *New York Times* headline read: "For a Modest Cardinal, a Farewell Full of Majesty."

There *was* something special about being around people who believed in something so strongly. By the time my mom's mom died, she was completely at peace with the fact that her life was ending. She had been a devout Catholic since she was a kid and seemed to just trust that heaven and everything else she had been praying for would be waiting for her when it was all over. I wondered a bit, too, if she was excited to see my grandfather again. I wished I could believe so strongly in something—but then again, I had my own "church": the church of adventure. (We're currently accepting members, FYI.)

Maybe it was my father's love of exploration and the outdoors, but I always felt most connected to him, and most spiritually alive, when I was out *living* . . . whether horseback riding in Langmusi, China; trekking on an elephant in Thailand; or watching the Great Migration in Tanzania. But mostly I felt him at the country house in the Berkshires, looking over the lake where we used to go sailing and knowing that if there is an afterlife, he'll be the first person to greet me when I get there. I thought about Gaby's question that day on Madison Avenue: what happens to us when we die? And I realized that I didn't have to believe in a heaven or have all the answers. I just needed to trust in my gut that my father was still here with me, in whatever way I needed him to be.

THE CATHOLICS were pretty straightforward with their funerals. A little prayer. A little standing up, and sitting down, and standing up again. The occasional kneel and song. You know, standard. The Hare Krishnas? They were a whole other ball game. My first Hare Krishna service was of, well, epic proportions. The body came straight from the hospital—a man, in his forties, who was almost *five hundred pounds*. He had died of a heart attack, a fact that was shocking to no one but sad nonetheless.

"We're going to need a double-wide casket for this one," whispered Tony.

There's actually a company called Goliath Casket (I swear) that makes coffins for the big-and-tall crowd. We didn't keep them on hand, so it had to be special-ordered. "I'll call them right away," I told him.

That's when the Hare Krishnas showed up. When I first saw the body, which was being kept in the prep room until the casket arrived, there was no way to tell who this person had been. He was just a man covered in a sheet—the hospital didn't bother to cover him more than that before putting him in a body bag. But as it turns out, he was a Krishna, and his friends were gathering outside Crawford, anxious to get inside and bathe him, which was their custom. Hare Krishna funerals, I learned, were pretty much the same as Hindu funerals. And that meant that before Bill did anything to the body, a ritualistic washing was in order.

"This guy is a Krishna?" I said to Bill in a low voice. Until then, most of the Hare Krishnas I'd encountered were people with shaved heads sitting on cardboard mats in

Union Square or the Columbus Circle subway stop, chanting and smiling as all of the miserable commuters gave them dirty looks. I don't know what I was expecting—flowers? Robes? Girls with tambourines?—but not *this*.

"Looks like it," said Bill. After decades in the funeral business, pretty much nothing could faze the man. It wasn't his first Hare Krishna rodeo.

"Aren't they supposed to be vegetarians?" I asked. "Have you ever seen a five-hundred-pound vegetarian?"

Bill laughed. "I don't know any vegetarians."

At Crawford, we were happy to accommodate any religious requests—and some pretty weird nonreligious requests—as long as it made the clients happy. So when the Hare Krishnas walked into the foyer asking to see the body so they could give it a bath, Bill led them downstairs. "Just give me a few minutes," he said, before disappearing into the embalming room. He had to clear out all the other bodies before they could come in and do their thing, not just for privacy's sake, but also because he didn't want water spraying all over the other corpses. That would have been terribly bad form.

This particular group of Krishnas was in normal clothes—simple, but nothing that made them stand out. Bill gave them aprons to put on and handed them a small stack of clean sponges. Usually he would close the prep room door, but the group seemed confused before they even started on the bath, so Bill decided to stay. It's a good thing

he did—they made a total mess of things! Not to play favorites, but the *chevra kadisha* Jews had the ritual baths down to
a science, barely a drop of water on the floor. This group? By
the time they were done, there were puddles—*puddles*—
everywhere, along with sandalwood, turmeric powder, and a
new cloth that had to be wrapped around the body. (Not a
super-easy thing to do with five hundred pounds of dead-
weight.)

Hare Krishnas tend to cremate bodies in simple coffins
shortly after death, so Bill had to move fast with the embalming process after the Krishnas left. "I can't find a vein,"
he said, hunched over the body. (The larger the person, the
harder it was to find a precious vein to use for embalming.)
"Come on, give me a vein, give me a vein. There we go!"

Bill made an incision and grasped a vein that led to the
heart. The pressure forced a flush of blood to the heart,
making it look like it was beating. "All cured!" he said.

"Bill!" I said. "Stop that!"

"I think we need some Otis!" he said, ignoring my fake
protest. A minute later, Bill was watching the embalming
fluid move through the clear tubes as Otis Redding sang
through the speakers.

The rest of the process went as normal, and Goliath had
speedily delivered the casket, so all that was left was actually
getting the body inside. We were all about death with dig-
nity, but there was no way around it: the only way to lift the
body into the casket was to use the hoist in the basement

that was *usually* used to raise the caskets themselves. Bill and I looked down as other staffers worked the mechanics, wanting to be respectful in such a moment. It was easy enough to laugh at all the craziness that went down inside Crawford, but at the end of the day, that body—that was a person. And someone loved him. Many people, maybe.

I was kind of hoping to plan a wild Krishna service, but no dice. A few prayers, a few chants, and the whole thing was over. I couldn't help but notice how calm, even relaxed, everyone was. Maybe it was because the Hare Krishnas, like the Hindus, believe in reincarnation. I kind of did, too. Gaby and I met when we were barely five years old, and I always felt like I had known her for much longer—like we were connected from a previous life. My mom shared the same belief, that there are certain souls that find each other in every life. Like, have you ever gotten off a plane in a new place and felt like you had been there before? Happens to me all the time. There is something reassuring about the idea that life runs in cycles; life, death, life, death, over and over, so that we don't actually lose people, we just meet them in another form.

MUCH MORE COMMON than the Hare Krishna service were the Jewish ones, this being New York City and all. I regularly recognized Elaine's friends from her synagogue (not that she was particularly religious, either) attending this service or that. "He had such chutzpah!" they'd say, shaking their heads in the back of the room. "A true mensch." Jewish funerals ran like clockwork . . . usually. With all the Jewish services Crawford and other funeral homes in town conducted, you'd *think* that no one would ever screw up the funeral for a prominent Jewish rabbi. And I guess they didn't, if we're being literal here. They screwed up way before that.

I was in my office when Bill knocked on the door. "You hear what happened over there?" he said, shaking his head. "Disaster."

"No! Tell me," I said. It had been a boring morning, and I was glad to have a little gossip . . . until I heard what it was.

"They embalmed a rabbi. What a mess."

I covered my mouth with my hands. Anyone who works at a funeral home knows that many Jews—especially conservative ones—don't get embalmed. So it was pretty clear that our colleagues had made a *big* whoops. "How the heck did that happen?" I asked.

"One of the guys over there, he made a mistake and wrote on the slip that the body should be embalmed," said Bill. "You know, idiot move. So without thinking, *Oh this is a rabbi, maybe I shouldn't pump him with chemicals*, the embalmer just went ahead and did what the paper said."

It was true that Jewish clients were starting to relax about a few things. It used to be that Jews would rarely be cremated, because of the belief that the messiah will come at some point and people will be resurrected. If you were cremated, you wouldn't have a body to come back in—which would be a shame, when all your friends were hanging out and you'd be missing the party. At least, that's one explanation. Some people focus more on Genesis 23, where Abraham went to great lengths to find a burial place, or "*achuzat kever*," for Sarah. For them, it's more about following tradition. Others simply don't believe in desecrating the body—lots of Jewish cemeteries won't even accept bodies with tattoos—and cremating falls under that category for them. But Reformed Jews, like my dad's side of the family, often weren't so literal. I guess like most things in religion, it was all open to interpretation.

Even though Dad was Jewish, we had his body cremated; a couple of years before he died, he mentioned that when the time came, that's what he wanted. It was one of the only details about his death that we ever talked about, and I was glad that we had. But it was really the *only* detail—Mom, Max, and I were left mostly in the dark when dealing with the rest of Dad's send-off, and we never actually discussed what he wanted us to do with the ashes. I wouldn't have been surprised if he had said to sprinkle them over the lake near the country house, or another spot that he loved. Or he might have been perfectly happy to stay just where he is now, in an urn on my mom's bedroom mantel. We just never got that far, or rather, we didn't want to go that far. It would mean acknowledging the fact that he was going to die—and that was terrifying. We weren't the only family to deal with a death in this way: I was shocked at how many people who came into Crawford had *no idea* what their loved one would have wanted. "We just didn't talk about it," they'd say, usually looking down at the floor, or up at the ceiling, as if an answer might suddenly appear from either. The more I heard that phrase, the more I questioned: *Why is it we are so afraid to talk about something as inevitable as death?* After over a year at Crawford, death no longer seemed scary to me, probably because it was no longer a mystery.

"THE PRIEST is here," said one of the guys who did removals for Crawford. He was walking to the back, where the smell of garlic was already wafting through the air.

"A priest?" I asked, chasing him down the hallway. "I thought this was a Muslim funeral." I looked down at the folder in my hand—yup, definitely Muslim. *Why would a priest be here?*

"Yeah, whoever, he's here," said the staffer. He had only been at Crawford for a few months, and we'd barely interacted.

I looked down the hall and saw the imam, patiently waiting by the reception desk while Monica avoided eye contact. She avoided dealing with visitors as much as she could and mostly got away with it. The union rules were locked pretty tight—it would have been hard to fire her, and weirdly, nobody seemed too concerned that she spent some afternoons napping on one of the couches in the chapel.

"That's not a priest, he's an imam," I told him. Maybe it was all my studies, but it bugged me when people refused to use terms from a religion or culture different from their own.

The staffer turned to me, annoyed at my correction. "Yeah, well, this is fucking America," he said. "Here, he's a priest."

Before I could correct the narrow-minded twerp on the fact that nationality had nothing to do with it, he had already disappeared into the back room. I turned my attention to the imam. Typically, Muslim funerals were very simple and to the point. They also did a ritual washing and wrapping of the body in a white cloth that looked like a sheet, à la the Hare Krishnas, but they were super efficient at it, à la the Jews. Muslims were almost never cremated; the most religious families, had they not lived in the US, where it's illegal, would have buried their loved ones without a casket even, laying them in the ground in just the sheet, with the head facing Mecca.

"It's a pleasure to see you again," I said to the imam. I recognized him from another service I had planned for a fabulous Muslim family whose daughter I had gone to private school with. Even though the $40,000-a-year school was historically Christian (the name was Trinity), about half of the students were Jewish, and a few were Muslim. We used to joke that the big cross hanging in the chapel was really just a "T" for Trinity.

"Same to you," he said with a smile.

I wondered if he had heard any of the comments from the staffer, who was probably now gorging himself with rigatoni.

"Should I take you to the viewing room?" I asked. Sometimes, priests, rabbis, or imams would say a few prayers before visitors arrived for a service.

"This priest would like that very much," he said, still smiling.

I felt myself blush. In 2004, when my father was sick and I was taking the subway between the NYU campus and the hospital every day, I used to read the Quran for class during each ride. (This was just a few years after 9/11, when New York was still unnerved, and as an unfortunate result, wary of Muslims.) I might not have been Muslim, but I had a lot of respect for the religion, and even learned a little Arabic through all of my readings. I hated to think that this imam might lump me in with other Crawford employees who were, shall we say, a little less open-minded. I couldn't blurt out, "I'm not like them! I know all about your religion! I've prayed in your mosques in India and Oman!" But I was deeply embarrassed at being associated with ignorance, much less intolerance.

Maybe it was because my father had always so openly embraced my mom's religion, or the fact that we only sporadically went to church, but I've always been fascinated with spirituality. And I never felt like I needed to pick just one faith. At my desk at Crawford, I had a statue of the god Shiva. I wore Buddhist prayer beads around my neck—I picked them up at a Buddhist monastery in Tibet. And, I regularly wore a ring that Ben had brought me back from Israel after Dad died. On the inside, in Hebrew, it read: "This too shall pass." I might not have been a stellar Catholic, but I was a spectacular optimist.

While a lot of my New York friends were atheists (a common trend in a city where people don't even make eye contact on the sidewalk), seeing so many families lean on God or some other higher power during their time of grief was starting to make a believer out of me. They say that when you experience the death of someone really close to you, you either reject God or get even closer to Him. (Or Her. Who's to say, really?) Don't get me wrong; my dad's death didn't make me want to go to mass every Sunday. But I did find myself talking to him out on jogs in Central Park, or randomly popping into churches or mosques to say a *berakhah* (a Jewish prayer) over a candle for him. It wasn't for show. Every part of me believed he was listening, even if God wasn't.

EIGHT

A Sorted Affair

$\mathcal{U}$p until the call came in, it had been a pretty slow morning. I said hello to Tony in his office, heard Monica saying my name in between whatever she was talking about in Spanish to the other receptionist (she was really starting to get to me), and made myself a green tea. We didn't have a service until late afternoon, so it was shaping up to be a bit of a snoozer.

And then, the phone rang.

Monica transferred the call to my office without notice because Tony was in a meeting, so I was going in blind. "This is Elizabeth, how can I help you?" I asked, taking out a pen so I could jot down notes for Tony.

It was silent for a moment. "This is Linda Pressman," said the woman on the other end. "My husband, Charles, died this morning."

"I'm so sorry for your loss," I said, meaning it. This was a call *nobody* wanted to make. I wanted Linda to feel as comfortable as she could. "Would you like to come in and arrange his service?"

Linda gave me the details: Charles, her husband, had died the night before on the way to a hospital on the Upper East Side. Heart attack. He was dead before the ambulance arrived at the ER, which was just blocks from their very fancy apartment building. (I recognized the address.) I told her we would take care of the transfer from the hospital—all she needed to do was come in at eleven o'clock and we'd walk her through everything. I wasn't happy for Linda's situation, but I was glad to at least have a client coming in to break up the day. For whatever reason, summer was our slow season—and it was the thick of August. I guess parties in the Hamptons and yacht trips to Martha's Vineyard were enough to keep the Crawford clientele living it up. Winter? We were usually booked solid. Tony said it was the total opposite in lower-income areas, where the heat seemed to stir up trouble on the streets and could be dangerous for the elderly. But Crawford didn't get that kind of business.

About an hour before Tony and I were expecting Linda, the red light on my phone lit up again. This time, it was *Sarah* Pressman. *What are the chances?* I thought as she said her name. Sarah told me she wanted to come in that afternoon, if possible, since she had to drive in from her house in Rye, New York, an affluent suburb. I started scribbling down the details about her husband, Chuck. "Heart attack? Oh, I'm so sorry for your loss. Cornell hospital? Sure, yes, we deal with transfers from there all the time. Can you come in this afternoon? We'll arrange everything."

It wasn't until I hung up the phone that it hit me: Linda Pressman. Sarah Pressman. Charles. Chuck. Heart attack. Cornell. *Oh my God*, I thought. *No.* I shot up from my seat and ran to the prep room to tell Bill, who I was praying could come up with an explanation. Instead, he let out a laugh. "I don't put anything past these people," he said, making a "crazy" motion with his finger.

"But it can't be, right? How could a guy be married to *two* women? And the second lady, Sarah, she mentioned they have a son!" I said, suddenly dreading the rest of my day. "It's not like Westchester is in *Siberia*. It's a twenty-minute drive away!"

"Sometimes people with money get away with crazy shit," said Bill. "Two wives? Two homes? Crazy fucking shit."

I walked back upstairs, pacing outside Tony's office. He was in there with the door closed, which meant he was with a client. I could feel Monica staring at me and heard her say my name again, which elicited a flurry of giggles from her front-desk posse. I'd never been someone who worried about what other people said about me; thirteen years in New York City private schools helps you build a pretty thick skin. (You know that movie *Cruel Intentions*? It was like that, minus the incest.) But Monica had it in for me from day *one*, and the fact that I couldn't understand what she was actually saying irked me that much more.

"If you're going to talk about me, as least have the guts to do it in English," I said.

"Oh look, Tony's princess is angry," said Monica. "Or should I say, Tony's girlfriend?"

"What the fuck are you talking about?" I said.

"You heard me," said Monica, smirking. "You must be doing something to get all his attention."

"This stupid, made-up drama, it's in your head," I said. "I've never been anything but nice to you, and I'm sorry if you don't like me, but you're just being rude now."

I knew Monica wasn't going to apologize—that would be asking too much. But she did at least shut up. Bill had told me that "the girls"(which is how he referred to the receptionists) had taken to calling me Princess, a totally obnoxious name considering I clocked more hours than all of them and did a lot more dirty work. (Monica could barely summon the energy to say hello to clients without mumbling.) Tony had heard as well, and he made a joke out of it by placing a flower stand next to his desk and calling it his Liz pedestal. Really, he was making fun of my short stature. But Monica and company didn't get the joke—and the silly gesture gave them something else to bitch about. A literal pedestal. Can you imagine the fuel *that* added to their fire? I could deal with being called a princess; it was obnoxious, but I had come to expect that from Monica. The girlfriend comment was just downright inappropriate . . . not to mention ridiculous.

After I spent twenty minutes walking back and forth, back and forth, Tony finally came out of his office. "I have to talk to you," I said, my stomach feeling queasy from the nerves. "Like, right now." It was almost ten fifteen, and we had to figure out what we were going to do before Linda arrived.

"Okay, let's talk in my office," he said.

I nodded and walked past him, ignoring whatever comment Monica was making from the front desk. *You don't have time for that BS right now*, I told myself.

I briefed Tony on the situation, waving both folders in front of him. "I don't know how to deal with this," I said.

Tony sighed and looked up at the ceiling for a second. He didn't look happy, but he wasn't panicking. *Shouldn't we be panicking?* I thought.

"I probably need to call her, right?" I said, still waiting for Tony to weigh in.

"This stuff happens sometimes," he said, shaking his head. "You got the number? I'll call and take care of it."

I pointed on the folders to where I had written down both Linda *and* Sarah Pressman's phone numbers and watched as Tony picked up the phone and dialed each of them separately. "Like a Band-Aid," he said. First, he spoke with Linda, telling her calmly that someone else had called in with the same information as she did. He didn't go on and on; he simply suggested that she come in that afternoon so that everyone could talk together and plan what felt most appropriate. Then he called Sarah and said pretty much the same thing.

"That's how it's done," he said. "These people, I tell ya."

"How did they take it?" I asked, genuinely concerned. I couldn't imagine ever getting a call like that. Now these women had to deal with not just the death of their husband but the fact that he was a two-timing jackass. "What did they say?" I couldn't imagine the same scenario happening again, but I wanted to learn how Tony had handled it.

"Not much," said Tony. "The goal of these conversations is to keep things short, calm, and make them feel like you have everything under control."

"Were they surprised?" I asked.

Tony shrugged. "I've been doing this a long time," he said. "Even when they don't know, they know."

The man had a point. By the time I was fourteen, my dad started taking me to parties with him. They were usually thrown by his clients, and he had to go show his face. Mom had zero interest in hanging out with a bunch of rap stars and music moguls, so Dad would take me. By that point, I had already seen my friends' fathers out to lunch with young, attractive women who were definitely *not* my friends' mothers. In Manhattan, there was always this sense of anonymity; in a big city, there's a decent chance you won't get caught slipping into a hotel or disguising a date as a "working lunch." But I was still shocked to see how many of his business acquaintances openly cheated on their wives, taking trips with their mistresses and barely caring if they were caught. Maybe it was all part of the arrangement: These women got to live the life of rich housewives, spending their afternoons shopping at Hermès and taking private yoga lessons. In exchange, they turned a blind eye when their husbands came home late . . . or not at all. My dad never addressed it with me, but he didn't really need to.

This was my first funeral with a man who was literally leading a double life—but I had already worked on more than a few services where it turned out that the guy in the casket practically had a PhD in philandering. At least in *those* cases, he hadn't gone ahead and married both of the women. But still, it was sad at one funeral to see the mistress who wasn't allowed into the wake for a man she had been seeing for eighteen years, even though more than a thousand other people were welcomed to pay respects. ("You are *not* part of the family," the man's son had yelled at the woman, while she stood crying in the foyer. His mother had paid for the funeral, so there was no way in hell "the other woman" was getting in.)

And it was downright surreal the day a man came in to preplan a service for himself, his wife, *and* his mistress. It was important to him to know that they would all be buried together whenever that time came. Why? No idea, although my guess was that he wanted to keep the love triangle going for as long as possible—for eternity, even. The weirdest thing about the guy wasn't so much his obsession with keeping the magic going; it was that he wouldn't shut up about his forty-two turtles. I'll say it again: *forty-two turtles*. If you ever doubted New York City was a fucked-up place, now you have proof. Yes, in New York City, even a man who hoards dozens of disgusting, disease-ridden reptiles in his bathroom can manage to seduce two women.

I was nervous waiting for Linda and Sarah to show up when Gaby texted me: STILL ON FOR TOMORROW?

Tuesday. Dinner. I had totally forgotten. Before I started working at Crawford, I used to host Tuesday dinner parties with my closest friends, plus Max and anyone else we knew who might be popping into town for a visit. I was stressed enough thinking about the meeting that afternoon, but I didn't want to disappoint my friends. SURE, WHY DON'T YOU COME OVER AROUND 8 ISH? I wrote back. I took a swig of coffee, desperate for some energy. *You can't cancel*, I told myself. *That would be super lame.* I had already turned down an invitation to go with Gaby on a private jet to the Caribbean. She understood—if anyone had come around on the whole me-working-with-dead-people thing, it was Gaby. But I still felt bad not having as much time as I once did for our wild adventures together. The least I could do was keep our dinner plans.

My stomach was in knots by the time one o'clock came

around. Linda was the first of the Pressmans to arrive. She was wearing a navy blue sheath dress and looked to be in her fifties, with short brown hair and enough of a tan to suggest a trip or two to the Hamptons. Even though she probably hadn't gotten a blip of sleep, she had managed to do her makeup and match her brown leather shoes to her classic Louis Vuitton tote. I was impressed.

"So sorry for your loss, Mrs. Pressman," I said, as usual.

She looked at me cautiously, like when you're walking through the Saks makeup counters in fear someone in a black suit and ponytail is going to jump out and spray you with perfume. "Thank you," she said. "Is, uh, is everyone here?"

"Not yet," I said, looking at my watch. "But let me introduce you to Tony and we can wait in his office."

Just as I turned around, in walked Sarah Pressman with a boy who looked to be eleven or twelve years old. Sarah was a little younger than Linda, maybe in her early forties. She was also a brunette—Charlie must not have been a blonde guy—but didn't have Linda's classic style. Instead of a cute dress, she was wearing khakis, sandals, and a white tennis shirt. She didn't have a lick of makeup on, and her eyes were swollen from crying.

There they were. Charlie's wives. Both of them. I watched in a certain horror as Linda took in Sarah and then the child. She and Charles never had children, but there she was, looking at his son. She took a sharp breath and clapped her feet together, as if to keep herself standing upright. Sarah was holding her son out in front of her like a shield, a hand on each of his shoulders.

"Hi," she said, finally. It could have been just seconds later, but it felt like hours. Even Monica was watching, like it was a soap opera.

"Hello," said Linda. Even though she was talking to Sarah, her eyes were fixed on the boy.

I figured this was my cue. "Now that everybody's here, let's sit down with Tony," I said, motioning toward his office. I looked at Monica, hoping that she might make herself even the *smallest* bit useful and set the kid up with crayons or something. But she was already walking back toward the break room, now that the dramatic moment had passed and there was nothing left to entertain her.

Tony walked out and shook both Linda's and Sarah's hands. Before he followed them into the office, I pulled him aside and suggested that maybe I should stay with the kid. We both looked toward the lobby, where he was sitting in a chair, looking at the floor. Pretty much nothing upset Tony anymore except seeing the kids left behind after a parent died, and there was high potential for this to be a, shall we say, "complicated" week for the family. "Go ahead," he said. "I'll take care of this and fill you in later."

I'll admit it: I was relieved not to be in that room. It didn't bother me so much that Charlie/Charles/Chuck had cheated—although it was certainly not ideal. I was bothered by the fact that he had done it so fully. He didn't have some quiet fling; he went out and had a whole other family. I couldn't imagine how Linda must have felt, seeing her husband's kid and not being his mother. If anything, Sarah at least had a piece of her husband through the child. Linda just had her memories, and even those were probably tainted now. Can you love someone if you didn't know a whole other part of their life even existed? Does that count as really even knowing them? I didn't know the answer, but I did have one idea: a scavenger hunt. The Crawford employee orientation video (yes, that actually existed) had specifically said not to play hide-and-seek with children in the funeral home—too much opportunity for a traumatic dead-body encounter—but it never mentioned scavenger hunts.

"What's your name?" I asked the boy.

He swung his legs under the chair, back and forth, back and forth. "Peter," he said, never taking his eyes up from the floor.

"Well, Peter, it's nice to meet you. I'm Liz. Do you want to play a game with me?"

Peter shook his head.

"Aw, please?" I said. "I need somebody to play with. It's a fun game, I promise."

There were no services going on until much later that day, so I made a short list of things Peter might find in the funeral home—mints, tissues, latex gloves, coffee cups. The kid had never played scavenger hunt before—I thought children in the suburbs *lived* for that kind of stuff—so I explained the rules and he quickly caught on. By the time Sarah and Linda were walking out of Tony's office an hour later, Peter had a paper cup filled with little "treasures" he had collected. Even Monica had given him one of her Sharpies in a rare moment of compassion. "Here, take a red one too," she'd said playfully. For a moment, I actually liked her. Well, sort of.

Charlie was Jewish, and so the funeral was the next day. I got to Crawford early, which had become my new norm. Only the *shomer* was there when I arrived. *Shomrim* were usually hired by Jewish families to act as a "watchman" of sorts; the idea is that a person's body must be guarded until it is buried. The *shomer* is also supposed to say prayers over the body, but on one occasion at our sister funeral home, a bunch of them were caught watching porn on the company computer. They weren't even savvy enough to delete the browsing history, and so when the web browser started autofilling with things like "free Asian hardcore" whenever someone typed "F," there was no denying what was going on. (It was also totally obvious who was doing the searching, since most of the activity happened overnight. The bosses were pretty sure the corpses weren't Googling porn.)

"Morning," I said to the *shomer*, dragging my bag into my office. Tony had taken over most of the arrangements for the Pressman funeral, but since I had initially taken the call, I wanted to be there to make sure everything was going according to plan.

Tony showed up an hour later. The plan was this: Linda Pressman would host a service for Charlie at ten thirty a.m. with her friends and family, and then Sarah would host a separate service that afternoon. The women each paid for a service but split the cost of the casket—and even though flowers aren't traditional at a Jewish funeral, they had them anyway, and split those too. The only official "swap" we would make was to very specific arrangements. For instance, we would wait to bring out the rose arrangement with a ribbon that said "Loving Father" until Sarah's service. The women also agreed not to divulge too much in the obituary. Usually, the last line included names of close family members—but they just left that blank. Charlie was "loved," but nobody was naming by whom.

After the first service—which went off without a hitch, despite my anxiety—Linda was supposed to go home and then come back after all of Sarah's guests left for the burial. But instead she lingered in the room, staring at her Charlie . . . who also happened to be someone *else's* Chuck. She was still in there when Sarah and Peter walked in to say their own private good-bye. "Should we do something?" I whispered to Tony. This was supposed to be Sarah's time—she had paid for it, and they had agreed.

"Let's just wait a minute," said Tony.

And then it happened: one of the moments of genuine compassion that can sometimes only happen at a funeral. Sarah invited Linda to stay. They didn't hug or anything, but the women looked at each other warmly, and Linda glanced at Peter with—I swear it—a look of love. He might not have been her son, but he was Charlie's son—and that was still something. Maybe real love isn't knowing everything about someone, but embracing the parts you do know wholeheartedly.

Linda spent most of the service lingering in the back. Nobody who came knew who she was, nor did they ask. Once the last of Sarah's guests left—she had requested a private burial, so everyone knew to skedaddle—she, Linda, and Peter got into a black limo and drove off to the cemetery. Who knows? Maybe each really did suspect the other had existed all those years. Maybe they loved Charlie enough, both of them, to ignore any suspicions. As crazy as it sounds, I was glad, in that moment, that Linda had Sarah. Sarah was the only other person who could understand *exactly* what she was going through. I wondered if the two would remain friends, or if the burial would be the end—a final good-bye after the final good-bye, each now knowing a little more about the man she'd loved.

BY THE TIME I got back to my apartment that night, it was seven thirty. I didn't even have time to change out of my black suit—my friends were coming over in half an hour. I had stopped at Lobel's, a small, upscale butcher near Crawford, and bought a roasted chicken I could possibly pass off as my own. I opened my fridge to see what

I could summon from the dead for a side. After a quick assessment, I decided the wilting vegetables I had ordered a week before on FreshDirect would have to do. I used to make more elaborate meals—rack of lamb with mint jelly, vegetarian lasagna with fresh garlic bread—but this was the best I could do at the moment. I hoped I could pull off a meal that would say, *Look how amazing I am at juggling my life!* but I had a sinking feeling that I would have been better off ordering sushi.

Gaby and Ben arrived together, with Max following fifteen minutes later. He had been working such late nights at the office, I was surprised he could make it at all. "And miss my chance to see my long-lost sister?" he joked. "Never."

"You're starting to sound like Elaine," I said, giving him a hug.

"If that were really true, I would politely request you just shoot me right now," he said.

"I won't worry until you start calling me lovey girl," I said. Even though I was exhausted, not to mention unnerved from the Pressman drama, it felt so *good* to be around family and friends again. I had been spending so much time consoling others' loved ones that it was sometimes hard to muster the energy to be there for the people *I* loved most.

"You guys won't believe the day I had," I told them, pouring us each a glass of wine. Ben grabbed the same corner of the couch he always did and pulled a cashmere blanket around his feet.

"Do tell!" he said in a fake WASPy accent. "Leave no detail out."

"No, I'm serious," I said, not seriously at all. "It was insane. We had two funerals for the same guy, because *both of his wives* wanted to have a service. He had two wives!"

Gaby was the only one who elicited the expected reaction. "*Oh my!* Are you serious?" she said, her big eyes growing even wider. "Why would someone even want that headache? I mean, it would just be so exhausting."

"You would think, but this went on for years," I said. "The guy somehow pulled it off."

Ben shrugged. "Dudes at the hedge fund do that stuff all the time," he said. (Ben was an up-and-comer at a large fund in Manhattan. Even at twenty-five, he was making more than a million a year.) "Pretty much any time we go out on a 'client dinner,' one of them is cheating on his wife. And girlfriends, it's like, forget it. Girlfriends don't even count."

I felt a small pang hearing the last line. A year earlier, I had dated a guy—I'll call him Carlo—who seemed like bad news from the get-go. He was beyond handsome—probably the hottest guy I had ever met—and while I'd never been lacking in confidence, even I thought, *Don't go near him, he'll totally cheat on you.* But Carlo was persistent; even though he worked eighteen-hour days at a hedge fund, he would cook late-night dinners and have a glass of wine already poured for me when I walked through the door. After we had been dating for a month—casually, or so I thought—

he took me to a bookstore, walked me to the travel section, and said, "Pick a place." I looked at him like he was nuts. He knew my fascination with travel; I kept a map where I actually crossed off places I had been and big circles over countries that were next on my list. But this was over the top.

"Oh my God, no," I said, smiling. The gesture was sweet, but a random trip to *anywhere* with a drop-dead gorgeous guy I barely knew?

"Come on," he said, tickling my side. "You're the girl who's up for anything. Well, here's your anything. Where should we go?"

I wanted to go somewhere he had never been as well, and so after a half hour of deliberation, we settled on Vienna. "Now let's go to your place and pack your bag," he said. "We're going tonight."

When we got back from Europe, my little fling with Carlo was turning into a full-fledged relationship. I kept telling myself that I needed to be careful, but even my guy friends said Carlo seemed like a winner, and I had to admit, he *was* a lot of fun. I was just starting to let my guard down when Carlo called one day to ask for the keys to the garage where I kept my bicycle. It was in my mom's building—I hadn't touched it since my dad got sick, since he and I used to ride together in Central Park. It was too painful. A reminder of my father's decline.

"I told you," I said. "I can't go in there. It's too hard."

"What if I bring your bicycle to *you* instead?" he said.

Later that afternoon, my buzzer rang, and there was Carlo standing on the sidewalk with my bike. He had had it cleaned—it looked better than when my dad bought it for me almost a decade earlier. I held back tears as I saw him standing there with it, and again as we rode through Central Park together.

About a week later, Ben called. "Liz, I have to tell you something," he said. His voice was so somber, I thought he was going to tell me someone had died. "And I hate that I have to call and tell you this, but as your friend, you need to know."

"Okay," I said, my heart sinking. *What happened that could be* this *bad?*

"Carlo cheated on you," he said. Just like that. No explanation, just four flat words that felt like a dagger.

"Okay," I said. *Liz, you expected this. You knew it would happen. You knew it all along.*

"I'm sorry," said Ben. He went on to describe how he knew: The woman Carlo had been hooking up with on the side was angry that he wouldn't commit to her. So she stole his phone and forwarded an e-mail Carlo had sent her—a very flirty e-mail—to all of my close friends. (We ran in the same circle, so Carlo had most of their contact info in previous group e-mails.)

"Send it to me," I said, hanging up the phone.

I took a deep breath when the e-mail popped up in my

inbox a minute later. It wasn't the message that bothered me, although it *did* make me a little queasy to have my suspicions about Carlo confirmed. What hurt most was the time stamp. It was marked at 3:40 p.m.—just twenty minutes before Carlo had been standing outside my building with my bike.

Does an e-mail count as cheating? Meh, that depends on the person. For me, the fact that Carlo could do something so sweet and so personal, and then, at almost the exact same time, flirt with another woman—that was the ultimate betrayal. A drunken kiss at a club, a playboy attitude—those wouldn't have hurt so much. I once broke up with a guy because of all the women constantly throwing themselves at him at parties. "But, Liz," he told me, "I would *never* cheat on you." I told him that it was just a matter of time, like a loaded gun in his pocket. As a joke, he bought me a necklace made out of bullets before I walked out his door and out of his life. That's just how it was: the people I knew were going out all the time. A generation of kids raised by doormen grew into a swarm of twentysomethings who barely knew what a healthy relationship even looked like. Parties and fund-raisers, fancy dinners and Tuesday-night black-tie galas—that was our world. Everyone was rich. Everyone was attractive. Add in an open bar, and, well, things happen. I was always realistic about that.

I plated the chicken and we moved over to the dining table. I was still in my black suit, although I had stripped off the panty hose, which were starting to make my legs itch.

"This is why I refuse to date anyone seriously," I said. "New York City men? Bunch of dirtbags."

"I take offense to that," said Max, pouring himself another glass. "By the way, these string beans taste like they need you to plan their funeral."

It wasn't that I never dated—I had been out with lots of guys and had been *mostly* lucky in love. Even my first relationship, which lasted through high school, was much deeper (and less dramatic) than you might expect. And since then, I'd had guys chase after me, all of them smart and sexy in their own ways. But the idea of settling into a relationship just to be comfortable, much less a risky relationship that might leave me deep into a pint of Ben & Jerry's and a *Sex and the City* marathon? No, thanks. I was perfectly happy to keep things casual, which just attracted the Upper East Side trust-fund babies even more. These were guys who were used to getting everything (and every woman) they wanted. The fact that I wasn't trying to pee in a circle around them to mark my territory seemed to make them even more interested. Also, I had close guy friends, like Ben, who were always there to be my plus-one at weddings and other events.

If I ever *was* going to spend my life with someone, I wanted the type of relationship my parents had. They were best friends. It's not the sweetest tale ever, but one story I always loved was the one my mom used to tell about her first married fight with my dad. She could never remember what the fight was about, but halfway through, she picked up a glass paperweight and positioned her arm like she might throw it. Dad barely flinched. "It looks like you're thinking about throwing that," he said calmly. "Before you do, you might want to consider that it's expensive, and breaking it might make you angrier. But it's up to you." Mom looked at the paperweight and started cracking up—and Dad followed suit. "That was our marriage," she said. Instead of cleaning out his whole closet when he died, she donated the suits but kept the sweaters for herself. She still wears them.

And I knew my dad would never have wanted me to settle. When I was a girl, I was obsessed with Gaby's mom's sapphire engagement ring. The thing could probably feed a small country, but it was stunning, not gaudy. "I want to get married so I can have a sapphire ring, too," a nine-year-old me told my dad one day. He put down the newspaper and looked at me sternly. "You don't marry for a ring," he said. "If you want a sapphire, I'll get you a sapphire. But you marry for love." He had never given my mom an engagement ring; she didn't want one, she wanted a watch. (Mom was practical like that.) Then about a year before Dad died, Mom was getting her watch fixed at a jeweler and saw the most beautiful emerald ring on a thin platinum band. "Try it on," I told her. "No, I can't," she said. "That's silly." A minute later, the ring was on her finger, and she had the biggest grin on her face. "No, no, no," she said, giving it back to the jeweler. "But it's lovely."

I told my dad that he had to go and buy Mom the ring;

she had been through so much taking care of him, and I also wanted her to have something special. She deserved it. But by the time Dad went to the jeweler, the ring had already sold. "Guess it wasn't meant to be," he nonchalantly told me. Then, almost a year later—by this time, Dad was in a wheelchair—he called to tell me he'd just received a message from the jeweler. The person who had purchased the ring couldn't finish the payments on it. The ring had been returned, and the jeweler wanted to know if Dad was still interested. "That's amazing!" I said. "I'll go pick it up for you."

"No," said Dad. "I want to do it myself. Will you wheel me over there?"

Christmas was a month later, and Dad and I couldn't pass out the presents fast enough. We left one huge box for last. "That one's for you, love," Dad said, pointing to it. (He couldn't walk across the room; he was too sick.) I'll never forget the look on my mom's face as she tore through the paper, opened the large cardboard box, and saw that little blue velvet ring box sitting on the bottom. She let out a gasp as she opened the lid to see the shiny emerald ring. "I love you," said Dad, smiling. Mom was in tears putting it on her finger. Dad died that March.

My mom and I had always had a complicated relationship, but after he died, she remembered the conversation my father had had with me when I was nine. "I want you to have what I had," she said. I didn't fully understand at the time—

Your husband is dead, I thought. *Why would you want that for me?* As if she could read my mind, Mom said, "I was happily married for almost forty years. Every time your father walked through the door, I was excited to see him. Not everybody gets that." She told me to get my coat and walked me to the jeweler, who had designed a ring just like hers, but with a sapphire stone. "From me and Dad," she said.

Max poured another glass of wine while I looked down at the ring on my finger. Even though Monica had been eyeing it at work—and maybe making all sorts of judgments—I didn't care; I wore it every day. Staring at it just then, I missed my mom. Even though she was close by and we called or texted each other a few times a week, things had been off ever since Dad died. I didn't know if it would ever feel like we were on the same wavelength again. My mind drifted to both Mrs. Pressmans. How did they find it in themselves to connect, even after being so betrayed? Maybe it was the fact that they had both loved, and they had both lost. Were Mom and I so different?

Gaby interrupted my reverie. "To health and happiness," she said, motioning for us to all clink glasses.

And love, I thought, raising my glass. *In all its complicated forms.*

NINE

I'll Have What She's Having

Elaine came to town. It wasn't to see me—although I was, as usual, a casualty of her visit. Her friend Barbara, another woman who wintered in Palm Beach and only spent warmer months in Manhattan, was finally ready to bury her husband's ashes. This sounds sweet, right? Like it was too hard for her to put him in the ground? Oh, no. Babs had requested that Crawford "hold on to him for a while" until party season was over in Palm Beach. She had been married to the man for *fifty years*, and yet she didn't want to miss a week of bridge or mahjong games to lay him to rest. And so there he stayed, in the walk-in-sized closet where we kept all the unclaimed ashes, some waiting to be picked up, some that had been there for, like, ever. I felt sad every time I walked by it, thinking of the people who had been left behind. Whenever I punched the code on the metal door to deliver an urn to a family member who'd finally showed up, I made it a point to say hello to all of the ashes and let them know they hadn't been forgotten.

After Elaine went to the service (which Tony handled; I wasn't involved, thank God), I met her at Aureole for lunch. The captain seated us on the top floor near the window, where Elaine was already slugging down a Smirnoff on the rocks with a twist of lime. When I was a girl, we used to meet for lunch at the Stanhope, which was a fancy hotel (and is now pricey apartments). It had a sidewalk café that was a hot spot for socialites—a place to "be seen," if you were into that sort of thing. If I wasn't in my prep school uniform—a green pinstriped jumper that was part dress code, part status symbol—my mom forced me into a smock dress. (Meals with Elaine were *never* casual.) Then Elaine would parade me around the dining room before taking a seat at the best table in the place. It was like she wanted everyone to see her perfect grandchild in a perfect dress with perfect, nauseating matching ribbons in her hair, even though normally I could be found in blue Umbro soccer shorts and a T-shirt. (Elaine didn't understand people who wore jeans, and she practically died at the sight of women in ballet flats or . . . gasp! . . . sneakers. Even the woman's slippers had wedge heels.) "Lovey girl," she would say, "do you know why this is called the *Stanhope*?" I would shake my head even though she had told me the story a million times. "Well, I'll tell you a funny story. When I was your age, I had a friend named Hope, and she had a brother named Stan. If you put two and two to-gether, well, do you understand? The couple who owned this hotel named it after their children! Stan. Hope." She was so proud that she knew these people, even though she probably hadn't spoken to Stan *or* Hope in decades. And that, ladies and gentlemen, was the Upper East Side.

"Your mother tells me you are still doing this . . . this . . . funeral thing," she said without looking at me as we perused the menu.

"Yup," I said, rubbing my finger over the mono-grammed clasp on my pearl necklace. Even now I found my-self playing dress-up to lunch with her.

"Well, I think it's been enough now," she said. "You re-belled. You played dead. Wonderful. Now, don't you think it's time you stopped embarrassing your mother?"

"Stopped embarrassing Mom, or stopped embarrassing you?" I said, raising my eyebrows.

Elaine let out a sigh of annoyance. "Your father worked so *hard*. You went to the *best* schools."

"Dad would be proud of me," I said.

"Well, Brett certainly had a mind of his own," she said, looking down.

For a second, I thought I saw a look of sadness on her face. *Could it be?* I thought. *Is she actually showing an ounce of grief for her dead son?*

"It's so hard, you know . . ." she started to say.

I leaned forward, completely shocked that Elaine and I

were about to have a heart-to-heart about Dad. I had never forgiven her for not coming to say good-bye to him at the hospital. Maybe, *maybe* this was our moment to heal from that.

"Yes, Nanny?" I said.

"It's so hard to know *what* to order in this place," she continued. "I really do miss the Stanhope."

YOU'D THINK that once people died, they'd quit the whole "Keeping up with the Joneses" routine and just rest in peace. And maybe they do . . . when they're actually dead. But one of the most lucrative parts of Crawford's business is the preplanning. People would come into Crawford, sometimes with an assistant or a notebook, and plan their own funerals. It sounds morbid, but this actually takes a lot of pressure off families to plan the perfect send-off for their parent or grandparent or whoever. And, perhaps for those who lunched at the Stanhope to "be seen," it also ensured that their memorial service would be up to snuff. If it was *really* done right, the service might even elicit envy. Can you imagine? As if all the Upper East Side biddies would stand over the casket, champagne in hand, saying, "Oh, dahling, this party is to *die* for."

The worst offense came in 2009. The economy was in the tank. Even New York City real estate prices had dipped, which is when you knew things were *really* bad.

There were Wall Street types walking around in a daze, BlackBerrys in hand, wondering what the hell to do after they'd just been laid off. For the first time in a *long* time, Crawford customers started asking about prices. "Can I get a discount on the casket?" "That is *way* too expensive for lilies. I know a guy who can get them for me for half of that." (Yeah, okay, buddy, like the guy who sells bundles of blooms at the bodega down the street is going to do the floral arrangements for your mom's wake.) Anyway, people started bargaining, sometimes in between tears. How someone has the clarity of mind to try to negotiate 10 percent off on a cremation the afternoon after their significant other died, I have no idea. What I do know is that money was draining out of the city, and if there's one thing rich people don't like, it's the feeling that their fortune is vanishing into thin air. *Poof.*

And yet, there were still women like Mrs. Divine, who came in to preplan their funerals, no expense spared. Lady Divine had been coming into Crawford ever since her husband died a couple of years before. The service, I heard, was a simple, elegant affair—no bells and whistles. So we were all a little curious when Mrs. Divine started asking about the priciest mausoleums, which can go for up to $300,000 at top cemeteries in the New York City area.

"She wants *what*?" I asked Tony. "Did you tell her the price?"

"Of course I did," said Tony. Actually, ever since 1984,

the Federal Trade Commission has had pretty strict rules on pricing so clients don't get scammed or surprised by funeral costs. If a customer asked about the price of something, we had to be very transparent, and all client meetings began with us handing over a general price list. No hidden fees, ever.

"And?"

"And she said no."

I was a little relieved to hear it. I had heard through the grapevine that Mrs. Divine was selling her apartment. Maybe the woman just wanted to downsize—totally possible. But there were plenty of people in Manhattan putting their pricey penthouses on the market, and I worried about an elderly widow willing to throw hundreds of thousands of dollars away on a glorified tombstone. "Well, that's good," I said.

Tony shook his head. "There's a big difference between a 'no' and a 'hell no,'" he said. "She was asking about the mausoleum that her friend—you know Mrs. Henderson, the lady who comes in here wanting to change her future funeral card all the time?"

I nodded.

"Well, she heard that Mrs. Henderson just secured herself a mausoleum in a beautiful plot by a tree, and she's not about to let her friend spend eternity in better real estate," he said.

"You've got to be kidding me," I said. Here I had been thinking Elaine was bad. This was off the charts.

The absurd cost of the mausoleum was the least of Mrs. Divine's problems in one-upping her friend in the afterlife. Mr. Divine had been buried in a plot next to where Mrs. Divine would be buried one day—and there simply wasn't enough room around them to fit a humongous shrine. So Mrs. Divine had come in to ask Tony if it would be possible to *un*bury (or "disinter," as we called it in the biz) her husband, have him cremated, and then use both plots to make room for the grand stone house that would put her friend's mausoleum to shame. (At least in her mind.)

"I've heard of people doing this," she told Tony, justifying her crazy. I don't know how he kept a straight face, but he did, and maybe the craziest part was that he was actually looking into the matter for her.

"You can't be serious," I said. Tony was no Bill—we didn't talk sports or rock out to Motown together. But I had grown comfortable enough to tell him when I saw a massive red flag waving in his face.

"We need the business," he said. He wasn't wrong: there had been increasing pressure from up high in the company to bring in more revenue. As far as I could tell, the Crawford staff had never had a problem selling overpriced funeral swag to clients—but I wondered if that was because the staff was oversimplifying the way they looked at money. To them, $90,000 for a casket was an *obscene* waste of money, but then again, so was $15,000, which is what the cheaper models at Crawford cost. The clients walking through the door, all with their designer clothes and chauffeurs waiting outside, looked pretty one-dimensional. The assumption was that since some people in the wealthiest parts of Manhattan could afford it, everyone could. It was almost not their fault . . . but Tony should have known better. I had noticed that he really worked clients during prearrangements. Maybe it was the fact that they were there to arrange their own service, and therefore might be willing to splurge on themselves. I'll admit it's not the worst idea, from a business perspective. But it still felt unnatural to peddle extras, like a sleazy broker selling an overpriced condo.

Despite the high cost of prearranging a funeral at Crawford, there were plenty of people lined up to do so. One was Mrs. Simon, who came in regularly, always with the red bag that she had used to take home the urn with her husband's ashes. She was an elderly French woman with a marvelous accent, and even though it was totally unnecessary for her to keep coming in—her funeral had been planned, and she had paid up-front—she liked to visit and "check in on things." One particular day, she was struggling to take her raincoat off, and she handed me the bag to hold for a moment. It was incredibly light, as though she were carting around nothing more than a bag of cotton balls. Which, as it turns out, wasn't far off.

I walked her into Tony's office, where she proceeded to pull a teddy bear from the bag and place it on his desk. Tony didn't flinch, but I was having trouble keeping a straight face. Was she giving him a gift? Had he seen the bear before?

"Nice to see you again, Mrs. Simon," Tony said.

"It's nice to see you too," she said, smiling. "I was wondering if I might be able to look at the different viewing room options again."

Tony went over the rooms with her, describing each briefly and then reminding Mrs. Simon that she had seen all of the rooms many, many times and they had decided on the perfect space for her service . . . whenever that might be. Then she asked about the flowers, and then the funeral cards, as if planning the event of the year. She was polite and lovely throughout the whole conversation, except that in between every question, she would turn to the teddy bear and ask what *he* thought she should do.

"Is she crazy?" I asked Tony after Mrs. Simon had put her raincoat back on and slipped out the front door. It was always sad to see people who were starting to lose it in their old age—which we got a lot of. "Does she think her husband's spirit is in that bear?"

Tony shrugged. "She's prepaid, that's what I know. As long as she has the cash, she can come in as many times as she wants," he said, walking back into his office and closing the door.

I'd learned a lot from Tony, but I couldn't understand his attitude. Prearrangements were important to business—I got that. But there had to be a better way of doing things, where Crawford could still meet its bottom line and be fair to customers. I wasn't sure what it was, but I was itching to find out. Unfortunately, I was beginning to think that Tony wouldn't be the one to teach me.

A COUPLE OF DAYS LATER, Tony called a staff meeting to make an announcement. Our sales were down. After months of clients requesting cremation instead of a burial (cremations tend to be much less pricey), one-day wakes instead of the traditional two, cheaper flowers, and fewer limos, our profits had taken a *big* hit. So in order to boost sales, Crawford was offering incentives to staff. Steak dinners. Trips to Cancún. All would be available to us, we were told, if we made our numbers from there on out. I tried not to roll my eyes. *Cancún? Is this really their answer?* It seemed that the higher-ups at Crawford's parent company had completely lost sight of what business we were in. Cheap perks felt desperate, and I started to wish I had taken a few finance or business courses in college so that I could offer a better solution.

At the end of Tony's little speech, we were told that as a last-minute reward for our hard work, we were going on a celebratory group trip to Montauk, New York. I had never been a fan of the Hamptons—the two-hour drive through traffic just to see the same people I ran into on Fifth Avenue was *not* appealing. (I was much happier to hole up in my family's country house in the Berkshires, looking out over the lake and enjoying being away from everyone.) Montauk was even farther east than the Hamptons, and not worth it, in my opinion. But not going would make me look like I wasn't part of a team, and I didn't want to give Monica free rein to tell stories about me by a bonfire, so I decided to go.

The company paid for a big house a few blocks from the beach, which was nice and all, but there was something weird about sleeping and eating and showering in the same space as two dozen of my coworkers. I let other people pick out their rooms and took the small room with a double bed on the first floor that was left over. It was no-frills, but I didn't expect frills. My goal was simply to survive the weekend and maybe even have a good time. Who doesn't like the beach, right?

Wrong. We arrived at the house around three o'clock. I kid you not, by eight p.m., most of the staff was drunk. And not like, "I'm going to adorably laugh at things that aren't really funny" or "Oops! I tripped on the sand!" shitfaced, but more like the seventeen-year-old girls who snuck into nightclubs and downed every shot of Goldschläger that pervy men bought for them until they could barely stand. By the time ten o'clock rolled around, the receptionists were grouped together gossiping, and the funeral directors were venting about all the pressure to make more money, and everyone was bitching about scheduling issues and who got to do what. I heard my name ring out a few times and felt myself pulling farther and farther away from the group until

I wasn't even in the light of the bonfire anymore. That was the thing at Crawford: people never actually talked through problems to say, "This is happening, how can we solve it?" Instead, everyone just complained behind each other's backs. The alcohol seemed to be breaking down those barriers, but not in a good way, and since Bill had plans with his kids that weekend, I didn't even have my usual ally to hang on the outskirts with. I desperately missed my own bed, in my own apartment.

"I'm not feeling so well," I told Tony, who was one of the few people not slurring his words. In fact, he had been nursing the same beer for over an hour. "I'm thinking of heading to the train station. Would you hate me?"

Tony looked at his watch. "I'm not letting a girl your age head home on the train by herself at this hour," he said. Even though our working relationship was full of wisecracks, there was still something fatherly about Tony, who actually did have two daughters around my age. "You want to go home in the morning? I'll drive you to the station."

"I could always take a cab," I said, although it was unlikely I'd find any car service willing to get me all the way out in Montauk at this hour.

"Just wait until morning, otherwise I'm going to be worried about you all night," he said. "I'll walk you back to the house."

"I can walk," I said, knowing it was only a few blocks. Then, in a lower voice, I added, "You-know-who's going to make a fuss if you walk me back. I swear, she's been staring at me all night."

Tony dusted sand off his legs and stood up. "Let Monica think what she wants. I'd rather her make up silly stories than have something happen to you on your way back to the house." The whole walk took less than ten minutes, and I sensed that Tony felt just as relieved as I did to be away from the group. "Wild crowd, huh?" he said, laughing, almost embarrassed. I laughed too. "Who knew?"

The next morning, I packed my monogrammed T. Anthony overnight bag and checked the train schedule on my phone. When I walked into the kitchen to make a cup of coffee before I left, Tony was already there, reading the newspaper. There was no food in the house—we had ordered pizzas the night before, and nobody had thought to bring bagels or anything for the morning. It was just a can of Folgers coffee that someone had grabbed from the back room at Crawford, plus a Ziploc bag of creamers and some sugar packets. I wondered if there was a Starbucks near the train station that might have better options.

"I think I'm going to head out," I told Tony.

"I'll drive you," he said. "The train ride's a few hours though. Let's grab breakfast before you go."

I certainly didn't have any better options, so Tony and I went to a small mom-and-pop-style café one block over. Even though there was nothing romantic going on, I was tired of Monica's snide comments. All it would take was a few people from the house venturing out for food (probably hungover) to make my life at work even worse. It was a strange thing; all of these people had worked together for years, some of them even decades, and yet it was old-school in the sense that the men talked to the men, and the women talked to the women. There wasn't much mixed socializing, which was maybe why Monica was convinced that my inter-action with Tony couldn't possibly be platonic.

As if on cue, Monica and two of the other receptionists walked by right as the waitress served up my fruit salad and rye toast.

"Oh Jesus," I said to Tony, turning my head away from the window. "Well, this is just great."

"You're worried too much about them," he said. "So they talk. Who fucking cares? Who cares what they think?"

I tried to block out Monica as Tony told me about the pressure he was under at work. I was surprised to have him open up to me, treating me more like an equal than an un-derling, but I also appreciated it. Big funerals were down, he said. People just weren't spending the money like they had been. He'd never seen anything like it in his more than thirty years in the business. There had been a brother and sister, he told me, who actually tried to save money on their dad's funeral by cutting words out of the obituary. (Charging by the word is standard.) People were still dying, and people were still being put to rest at Crawford—but nothing like before. I thought about the $150,000 funeral I had planned for Dr. Feelgood the previous year. It was true: families who might have spent that kind of money were now spending half that amount, no matter what their net worth was. As I listened to Tony vent, I better understood the intense pressure he'd been under for months, if not longer. It was his job to keep the ship afloat, and even if I didn't agree with all of his business tactics, I sympathized with the stress hanging over him.

"We're really relying on the preplan stuff," said Tony, sipping his third cup of coffee.

"Well, there was that one lady who came in," I reminded him. "Ruth? Remember her? She fell down in her apartment and said that the knock on her head made her realize she should get her funeral in order."

"Maybe you can do some research when you get back," said Tony. "Take a look at the numbers across the country. See if we're down more than the others. I can't believe I'm even saying that; we're talking about Manhattan, for Christ's sake."

When I got home that afternoon—I was so glad to be back, you'd have thought I'd just spent the night in prison—I researched sales figures for funeral homes in different states. With the whole country in a recession, Crawford certainly wasn't the only funeral home taking a hit. One family-owned business in Ohio got so desperate for money, they actually gambled away the preplanning funds hoping for a big win that would take them out of the red.

They weren't the only funeral home to think of this, either. While Bernie Madoff was burning up his investors' life savings, these guys were also making bets with other people's money. Stories like this no longer shocked me. I'd never thought about money more than when working at Crawford—everyone around me had always just *had* it. Maybe it was the funeral business, maybe it was business in general, maybe it was the tanking economy. All I knew was that the whole world seemed to be grasping for increasingly limited dollars, and it made me uncomfortable, even a little sad.

PRETTY SOON, the only thing Crawford staffers asked each other after a meeting with a client was, "How much did the family spend?" Everyone was on edge, and some of the union workers started talking about layoffs and who would be the first to go. The way the rules worked, the newest person to each rank was technically supposed to be fired before people at the same rank with seniority. As far as the union was concerned, I was still a receptionist. My title, director of family services, was recognized by Tony— and by our clients—but the union wouldn't give a subway rat's ass.

"Do you think I should be worried?" I asked Bill, who was busy coating a woman's nails with a polish from Chanel's fall line.

"The only thing you should be worried about is Eli

Manning. It would be nice if he could throw the ball to somebody on his own team for a change," said Bill.

I wasn't in the mood to talk football. As much as I didn't *need* the job at Crawford, it was the only place I felt like I had a real purpose, and I wanted to be doing something that mattered. Here, I could help people, be there for them in their worst moment . . . and maybe make it suck a little bit less. It was meaningful work, even if it wasn't always so glamorous. And while I knew I wouldn't work at Crawford forever—I saw it more as a place to learn the ropes—I was nervous about starting over somewhere new. I wasn't ready for that. Not yet.

"Don't look so down, kiddo," said Bill. "Hey, I've got a story that will cheer you up."

"Oh yeah?" I said. "I'm all ears."

Bill went on to tell me about a woman who had come in that morning with a very, uh, *special* request. Her husband had died two days before, and she had called in a panic saying that she wanted to come retrieve something off his body and that she only wanted to talk to the embalmer. Bill was never on the phones, but they pulled him out of the prep room to take the call. He could barely hold it together when the woman—who was in her late seventies, mind you—said that she wanted to pick up her husband's penis pump, and could he please discreetly remove it for her. This wasn't some air-pump apparatus still attached to his you-know-what. The man hadn't died midsqueeze. The pump had been surgically implanted into his penis and she wanted Bill to *take it out* and wrap it up so that she could take it home.

"Oh my God," I said, laughing. "What could she possibly want it for?"

Bill was practically in hysterics. "Exactly! What's she going to do, give it to her new boyfriend at the senior center?"

"Do you even know how to . . . you know . . . take it out?"

Bill's whole back was shaking from laughter. "No idea! But I guess it doesn't really matter. It's not like the guy is going to need his man parts again, and I'm pretty sure nobody at the wake is going to pull his pants down."

"How are you going to give it to her?" I asked. "What will you even put it in?"

Bill pointed to a box of Ziploc bags. "I was thinking those. I'll wrap it in paper towels first, and then seal it nice and tight."

"Stop," I said, now also in hysterics.

"Like I always say, can't make this shit up."

While Bill finished the body he was working on—and then dealt with the penis-pump situation, a show I did not need to attend—I went back up to my office to go over folders. I was only halfway through the first one when my phone rang. There was a man there to preplan the funeral for his sick wife. She had been ill for months, and while she was still hanging on, he wanted to get the arrangements out of the way. This wasn't abnormal for the terminally ill; sometimes, families just wanted one thing off their plate, or to busy themselves in a stressful time. I was glad the call had come to me—at least I could help make sure he was treated with compassion.

Some clients walked through the Crawford front door almost stoically, taking a very businesslike approach. For them, it was easier to look at this as a simple transaction and not focus on the loss of their loved one, and I could understand that. Others wore their grief more visibly—especially clients who had been helping a loved one through a long illness. It was sadness, fatigue, and relief all rolled into one. It was also immediately recognizable.

Mr. Roberts fell into the second camp. He looked to be in his eighties and was wearing a full suit—which was formal for someone just coming in to do some preplanning. I didn't know all of the specifics, like what his wife's condition was, but I knew by looking at him that he was in pain.

"I was told you could help me, Elizabeth," he said in a soft voice. I'd never known either of my grandfathers, but he had that look about him that said he would have been the type to take his grandkids out for ice cream, even before dinner. There was something so kind about his demeanor, which made me feel even worse about what he was going through.

"Yes, please, take a seat," I told him. "I'm so sorry to hear about your wife."

And then Mr. Roberts surprised me. He shook his head. "Don't be sorry," he said to me. "You don't grieve a good life. And she had a good life. *We* had a good life."

It was a philosophy that was almost Buddhist and reso-nated with me completely. Yes, he was sad that his wife was dying . . . but it wasn't a loss. They were married for sixty years, he went on to tell me, and loved each other through all of them. I had to bite the inside of my cheek to keep from tearing up as he described his wife, whom he referred to as "my girl," and how he would be happy for *her* when she didn't have to live in a failing body anymore. As he contin-ued talking, I got the sense that his wife was perhaps in her last days, even hours. A day earlier, a priest had come to the house, he said, to perform last rites.

I asked him just a few questions: how many people might attend, her favorite flower, if they had any children or grandchildren who might want to do something as a special tribute during the service. Then I told him to go home to her. "We'll take care of all of this, and when you give me a call, we'll have everything ready," I told him, squeezing his hand.

The call came four hours later. As fate would have it, Mr. Roberts "got a feeling" on his walk home from Craw-ford and picked up the pace. He walked into the door of the bedroom where his wife was resting—the same bedroom they had shared for almost their entire life together, he later told me—and rushed to her side. They looked at each other one last time before she closed her eyes for good. When I heard the story, I felt a sense of pride. Mr. Roberts had come to Crawford to calmly plan his wife's funeral before she died. He was able to focus completely on her in her final moments, which is exactly how it should be. That was why I was at Crawford in the first place, and it felt good to leave work knowing I'd done my job right. Still, I couldn't help but think, *What if I hadn't been the one to pick up the phone?*

TEN

Foreign Diplomacy

$\mathcal{I}$f there were one golden rule of funeral planning, it would be this: do not lose the body. You can fuck up pretty much anything else, but just like there is no murder without a body, there is no funeral without a body. It's kind of the main event.

You know where this is going. I lost a body. Not just *any* body, but an African ambassador who had been working at the United Nations. He was a VIP in the political world, but he was also the husband of my mother's friend. And he was gone. Because of me.

Crawford had a deal with the UN that whenever a foreign dignitary died, the body would be brought to us, where an embalmer would prep it or the body would be cremated, and then we'd ship it to the home country of the deceased. I had seen Tony work on several of these cases before. After

Bill worked his magic, the body was placed in a casket and then a wooden shipping container. Before we sealed the container, a representative from whichever country the person hailed from would come to make sure that nothing that was supposed to be in the casket was missing and that there weren't any items enclosed that weren't supposed to be there. The differences in how representatives from around the world handled this task was almost like a cartoon. The Italian representative who came once was all, "Hey! Looks great! Send him off!" while a Russian representative took a much more serious approach. The guy was wearing one of those fur caps that are flat on the top and have flaps over the ears—it wasn't even that cold outside—and had a stiff expression. He *obsessed* over the casket, checking out every detail of the body and that it was laid out just right with the proper clothing and who even knows what else. It was almost thirty minutes before he finally stepped back, nodded, and supervised the container being loaded into a hearse. I was surprised he didn't inspect the vehicle, too.

I had just finished sipping my Dean & DeLuca latte in the back room when I got word that the body of the ambassador was being brought in. The death had been sudden—heart attack—and so Bill was waiting for someone from the family or the UN to arrive and drop off clothes to dress the body in. I was curious about who, exactly, Mr. Ambassador was, and so I walked into Tony's office to see if I could read the folder.

"Oh gosh," I said, looking at the name. "I think my mother knows this family." I vaguely recognized it from my mom's building. There wasn't a ton of social interaction between residents, but pleasant "hello's" and "nice to meet you's" were standard.

Tony explained that we needed to arrange to ship the body to Africa that day, since the family had planned the funeral for just two days later. There were no direct flights, so the plan was to fly the ambassador to Paris, where the body would need to be escorted off the plane and someone from the UN would need to walk with it to make sure it was properly transferred to *another* plane, which would take it to Africa. (I won't name the specific country, to protect the identity of the ambassador.) I made it my absolute *mission* to see that this body got there safely. There were a lot of politics involved—and a lot of precautions. *Don't write "UN" anywhere on the container, or someone might steal it.* (This actually happens, especially in less-than-stable countries where thieves can ransom a dead body.) *Make sure there's someone at each layover to oversee the movement of the box. Check how much the casket weighs; if it's too heavy, it won't be able to go on the smaller plane for the last leg of the trip.* I checked all the boxes—double-checked them, even—and started mentally designing my superhero funeral-planner costume.

The morning went as it was supposed to: Bill did his

usual embalming and prep work, someone from the UN came to check things out and give us the go-ahead to ship, and the body was brought to the airport and loaded on a plane as cargo. (This is totally normal—chances are, you've flown on a plane with a corpse next to your luggage. Luckily, dead people aren't fussy travelers.) The rest of the day was normal—a little slow, even. I got a call in the morning saying the body had successfully made it on the plane and was en route, and with that out of the way, I spent much of the afternoon searching for the perfect gourmet chocolates from La Maison du Chocolat to serve at a funeral for a woman who had had a deep affection for fine wine and rich sweets.

I was about to leave for the day when my cell phone rang. It was my mom, which wouldn't have been weird except she rarely called me during the day when I was working. "Elizabeth," she said in a no-nonsense tone. "I just got a call from my neighbor two floors down. She said her husband—he's an ambassador, have you seen him before?—was brought to Crawford. She was supposed to get a call when the body landed in Paris, but there hasn't been a call. They don't know where the body is, and the family is waiting. I told her my daughter works at Crawford and that you can help."

I saw my night of relaxing with a bottle of Sancerre vanishing before my eyes. "Well, I'm sure the body isn't, like, *missing*," I said, praying that I could resolve the problem quickly. I was exhausted, and the last thing I needed was more work drama, let alone work drama that involved my mom. "Let me see what the deal is."

Tony wasn't in his office, so I walked down to reception to find him standing next to Monica, yelling at the phone.

"Everything okay here?" I said.

"We're trying to call the fucking airline in Paris and the phone won't connect or something," said Tony, turning red.

It hardly seemed possible that the phone was personally refusing to connect to Paris. "Well, are you dialing the country code first?" I said.

"What the fuck are you talking about?" said Monica.

I sighed. "You have to dial zero-thirty-three before the number," I said.

Monica dialed again, and after what must have been a full minute of rings, someone from the airline finally picked up. "I have no clue what this guy is saying," said Monica, frustrated.

"He's speaking French," I said. "Here, give me the phone."

I may not have known what Monica had been saying about me in Spanish all that time, but I was the only person on staff who knew how to speak any French. I asked the airline representative if she could pass me to someone higher up on the food chain, and after another ten minutes of waiting, I eventually got to the night-shift manager, who had absolutely no idea where the body was.

And that's when I started to panic.

By the time nine p.m. rolled around, I had put calls in to the UN and the security staff at Charles de Gaulle Airport. I even Googled language nuances that I never learned in French class to make sure. Was there a difference between how you say "a body" and "a *dead* body"? Turns out, yes; a body is a "*corps*" and a corpse is a "*cadavre*." A missing *corps* could mean a man was wandering the airport, lost. A missing *cadavre* was a code-red emergency . . . especially when said *cadavre* was a foreign dignitary.

Mom started texting me: DO YOU HAVE ANY INFORMATION? THE FAMILY IS WAITING AT THE AIRPORT IN AFRICA AND THERE'S NO INFORMATION COMING IN. PLEASE HELP. I TOLD THEM YOU COULD FIX THIS.

Oh, no pressure, I thought, putting my phone back in my pocket. In addition to finding the missing ambassador, I also had to deal with Mom, who had finally found a reason to care about my job. It was frustrating that the first time she was taking a sincere interest in my life at Crawford was when one of *her* acquaintances needed a hand, but that didn't change the fact that this was my chance to prove to my mom that my funeral gig wasn't silly or beneath me—when an ambassador dies, you want to have someone you can call who you *know* can take care of things. And ta-da! That person was me.

"What's the update?" said Tony. It was looking to be a late night for both of us.

"I'm calling everywhere I can," I said. "But it's late, it's not an easy time to get people on the phone."

"It's only nine!" said Tony.

Is this my life? This is my life. "Um, well, it's nine *here*, but it's three in the morning in Paris," I said.

Tony told me to keep calling, and so I did, trying to stay calm on the outside while my mind went straight-up frantic. I needed to get it right. "Think, Lizzie," I said, pacing around my office. I thought of the layout of Charles de Gaulle Airport; I had rushed through it dozens of times on quick trips to Paris or on stopovers to other countries. *Where could a body be hiding?*

I finally connected to the relative who was supposed to meet the body in Paris to fly with it to Africa, where the rest of the ambassador's family was waiting (and starting to freak out). The only problem? He had zero information. He didn't even know for sure if the body was still in Paris, or the flight number for the plane that was *supposed* to take His Excellency to Africa.

I will figure this out, I told myself, taking a deep breath. When the ambassador's son called saying that the small plane his father should have been on had landed, and they were all at the airport wondering what the hell was going on, I knew I had to stay calm. If he sensed I didn't have the situation under control, he would (understandably) feel more and more uneasy. I'd visited Tanzania and South Africa, and even in well-developed areas, there could be a lot of corruption and random shit going on. I remembered landing in Johannesburg and handing my bags to two gentlemen wearing badges that said "airport security" on them. My driver jumped in between us and grabbed the bags back, telling me that those men didn't actually work at the airport—they were there to steal foreigners' luggage. All of the locals knew this like it was no big thing, and I wondered, *Well then why the hell doesn't someone kick them out of the airport?* Every country had its own limits on what it was willing to put up with, I guess. That, or they had bigger fish to fry than protecting my suitcases from a bunch of crooks.

By eleven p.m., I realized I might have to take this to the government level. There was a real chance the body wasn't so much *lost* as it was stolen, in which case, I was going to have some major answering to do, not just to Tony, but to my mom. I had done everything I could to make sure the ambassador arrived safely; it just wasn't enough. Now, from across the Atlantic, I was supposed to clean up the mess.

Most of the lights were out at Crawford, with Tony and I working from our separate offices. He didn't speak French, so he couldn't make any calls—but he also refused to leave without knowing that the situation was taken care of. "We can't afford to fuck this up," he said, scratching his head in my doorway. "If people hear about this, we could lose business. We can't lose any business."

"I promise that I'm working on it," I said, annoyed that

Tony was talking money when someone's loved one had gone missing.

As shifts at the airport changed, I finally called and got transferred to an airline representative who knew what he was talking about. He personally worked with security to confirm that the casket hadn't arrived in time on the other flight, but it was safe in storage at the airport and would be loaded onto another plane to where the family was waiting. Hearing that everything was going to be okay made me want to cross the ocean myself and throw my arms around him in gratitude.

Since the ambassador was from a relatively remote area, there weren't regularly scheduled flights, the way you can just hop on a plane to London pretty much any minute of the day. Maybe, *maybe* one plane went out there a day—and that wasn't a guarantee. But my new best friend at the airline said that it was no big deal, they were scheduling another flight and would be loading the ambassador shortly.

The first person I called was the ambassador's son, who I knew would be relieved. "The body is on its way," I said, super grateful that I wasn't instead calling him to say, "Oh hey, yeah, I have no clue. Best of luck!" He thanked me profusely, finally sounding calm. Due to the time difference, the funeral was scheduled for just twelve hours later at this point, and the flight would eat up at least half of that—and that's not counting loading and taxiing time.

Then I called my mom, even though it was the wee hours of the morning. My hands shook as I pulled up her name in my contacts list. Part of it was the caffeine—I had been up for twenty hours, fueled mostly by coffee. (I'd even gotten desperate enough to drink the crap they kept in the back room, along with the powdered creamer.) But it was also adrenaline. I had done it. I had lost the body—but more importantly, I found it. Problem solved.

"Hi, Mom," I said, trying to sound businessy, like I was talking to a client. "I wanted to let you know that the ambassador's body is en route and the family has been notified."

"That's great news, Elizabeth," Mom said in a groggy voice, like she hadn't been sleeping either. I waited for more, wanting to hear her say that I had done a good job and she could see it all clearly now—why I was good at this, how it wasn't so crazy after all. But she didn't say anything else.

"So I guess you can call your neighbor, or whatever," I said. I felt defeated, like it would never be enough.

Just as I was about to hang up the phone, Mom said, "Who would have thought all those years of French would pay off for more than just ordering at La Grenouille?"

I tried my best to laugh. I knew she was trying—but why couldn't she just tell me that she was proud of me, that I had done well?

"You know, Elizabeth, this funeral thing, it's not that I haven't supported you," she finally said after a few seconds of awkward silence. "I just don't want you to become . . . so . . . so . . . *morbid*. You deserve to have a happy life. I *want* you to have a happy life."

"I am happy," I said. For the pittance I was making, my job was less a job and more charity work for the Upper East Side. There was no way I would do it—or even could do it—if it weren't gratifying in its own warped way. My mom must have known that, somewhere deep down.

We said good night, even though it was technically morning. I hung around Crawford until we got the call that the body had landed in Africa, one hour before the funeral. By that point, I was technically supposed to be back at work in two hours, but instead Tony sent me home—maybe because he felt bad for me, but maybe also to save a little overtime money. I had unexpectedly worked two back-to-back shifts, my adrenaline rushing for hours on end. Instead of feeling burned out, I was completely wired. And so I found myself walking past my apartment and farther downtown until I was standing outside of Gaby's building. I texted her: ANY CHANCE YOU'RE UP?

Gaby texted back: JUST LEAVING BUNGALOW! SHOULD BE HOME IN 10.

Of course you are, I thought, smiling. My life had changed so much. This *job* had changed me so much. For so many years, I was right there with her, coming home as the sun came up and sleeping off whatever I'd been drinking until half the day was gone. Part of me missed how carefree it had all once felt—nights filled with champagne and club music instead of chaotic phone calls to locate missing bodies.

Gaby eventually pulled up in a cab, stepping out onto the

sidewalk in a short purple dress, red lipstick, and big glasses that looked clunky and yet adorable on her narrow face.

"Lizzieeeee!" she said, giving me a hug. She smelled like perfume and smoke—it was a scent I remembered too well, and just having my nose near her hair brought me back to all of the crazy nights we'd spent together. "I was just thinking about you. This must be a sign, we are supposed to be together right now." Then she gave me the once-over, taking in my grandma-esque flats, black pants, black blazer, and what I'm *sure* was hair and makeup that looked like I'd just had a rager of my own.

"Long night?" she said.

I put my arm around her. "Not as long as yours, apparently."

We went inside, made a pot of green tea and a pan of organic scrambled eggs, and collapsed on her bed. "Tonight was crazy," she said. "We miss you! When are you going to start coming out again?"

I kicked my shoes off and pulled a blanket up over my legs. I didn't actually know how it would all end or what my next step would be. But what would have happened if I hadn't been there to talk to the airline staff, UN representatives, and airport security? Would the body still be missing? Would Monica *still* be trying to figure how to dial out of the country? Nobody on the outside knew what a mess Crawford could be under the surface—but I did. I was the one person who could see both sides.

"When people stop dying, I guess," I said, smushing my face into a pillow. Now that I had eaten something, the exhaustion was starting to kick in. Pretty soon, it would be a full ache.

"Well, that's not very optimistic," said Gaby, who was now also under the covers. "Hey, want to watch *Breakfast at Tiffany's* for the millionth time?"

"That sounds perfect," I said. Before Audrey Hepburn finished her pastry, I was fast asleep.

ELEVEN

One Last Hit

*M*ost of the time, it was a major plus that I had so many connections in Manhattan. Nobody else at Crawford knew the clients the way I did, and it was a major career booster that I had heard of—or partied with—many of the clients who walked through our door. But there were moments when I wished I weren't quite so close to them, like the morning my phone rang at five a.m., my friend Tom's name flashing on the screen.

Let me say this: *Nobody* calls at five a.m. because something awesome happened. There's no, "I got engaged!" or "I got promoted!" five a.m. phone call. No no. This particular hour is reserved only for news so horrible, it can't wait another hour until the sun comes up. Seriously, I will give you a dollar if anyone has ever called you at five in the morning to tell you something that didn't make you cry.

So when my phone buzzed, I immediately knew it was bad. Tom owned one of the hottest clubs in Vegas, and I had partied with him on many random weekends that called for a last-minute trip across the country to do nothing but sip comped bottles of champagne and dance poolside. (I never actually went in the pool, which was usually filled with so many beautiful people hooking up, you'd pretty much be *asking* to get herpes just sticking your toe in.) He was a businessman, and he was successful—but he also knew how to get into trouble.

"Who died?" I said, not even bothering to say hello.

"Lizzie," he said, his voice shaking.

"Tom? Tell me. What happened? Who is it?"

All I could hear was Tom crying into the other end of the phone. There I was, in the dark, sitting up against a mountain of pillows and waiting to hear.

"Tom," I said, my voice a flat whisper. "Say it." My mind started to race through our shared friends. *Was Gaby in Vegas this weekend?* I thought, starting to panic. *Please don't be Gaby. Oh my God, please*, I thought.

Tom cried into the phone, making muffled sniffling sounds. "Sam," he said, pain seeping through his voice. Then, even louder, "Fuck! It's Sam. We're thinking overdose. They found him loaded up with painkillers."

Sam was a famous musician, not just in Vegas, but around the world. You've heard Sam's music. You've danced to Sam's music. You may have even rolled to Sam's music (no judgment). I had heard through mutual friends that he had been struggling with painkillers, but with so many drugs being passed around clubs and parties, it was hard to say who was using and who was just . . . there. Plus Sam wasn't like all the trust-fund babies I had partied with over the years—he had worked his way up and made it to the top of his business all on his own. There was no platinum card that Daddy was paying off every month, no sense of entitlement. Sam actually worked for a living, and while he might have taken pills here and there, it seemed like he wouldn't risk more than a hangover maybe, or a bad headache. Certainly not *death*. I clutched the phone in my hand, replaying Tom's words in my head, feeling more and more disbelief as they sunk in.

"What?" I said, almost in a whisper. I tried to block the images flooding my mind—Sam alone on the floor, Sam going numb, Sam closing his eyes. I didn't know what had happened, but I could envision it. Some of the younger faces I'd seen at Crawford, exposed in open caskets, came rushing at me, and I fought to push them out.

"I don't know what to do," said Tom, still crying. "What the fuck do I do?"

I thought back to all the crazy nights I'd spent in Vegas. They were like scenes out of a Todd Phillips movie—like the time Tom flew in strippers from LA, because he claimed the ones in Vegas weren't "hot enough." Tom always set us up with the penthouse apartment at the Encore, with unlimited

Cristal, catered meals, and a personal butler to fetch any-thing we wanted. It was all-out excess, all the time, and after three days I was usually ready to plop my body into a first-class seat on the plane and sleep off the booze and steaks and dance music still playing—*thud, thud, thud*—in my head. It was completely lost on me how Tom could *live* there.

"I'm booking a flight," I told Tom.

"No, that's the thing," Tom said. "Sam was in New York. He had some meeting on Thursday and decided to stay for a few days."

"In that case, all you have to do is give me the address," I said.

THE SERVICE would be in California. It was where Sam had been living the past few years, and most of his family and friends were on the West Coast. But since you can't just cover a dead body up in bubble wrap and ship it across the country—it would be a rotting mess by the time it arrived—I arranged to have Sam taken to Crawford to be embalmed. Just as with the ambassador, it was common for some of our wealthiest clients to request a body to be shipped. Many had family plots in Europe or Asia where they wanted loved ones to be buried after a service in New York.

I made sure I was at Crawford at seven a.m. so I would be there when Sam's body arrived. Even though there was nothing I could really do, I wanted to know firsthand that everything was under control. Shortly after I got there, Sam's publicist released a statement about his death. I knew it couldn't be too long until the paparazzi were lined up outside with their cameras, hoping to get a shot of Sam in a body bag or a coffin. I did what we always did when a famous person was brought into Crawford: I reminded the receptionists not to give out any information, not even to confirm he was here. I asked two of the part-time staffers to put barricades out front so that other clients wouldn't be disturbed when the media showed up, and I told one of the receptionists to approach *anyone* who came into the foyer, just in case a reporter was trying to pose as a family member or a lost tourist.

Sam's body was delivered without incident, thank God, and brought right into the prep room, where Bill was waiting in his apron and gloves. I watched as Bill unzipped the body bag and moved Sam to a table. He was still in the jeans and T-shirt he had been wearing when he died, and had his usual facial stubble. I had seen over a hundred dead bodies, but I couldn't shake the sadness that had come over me seeing him there. Sam wasn't one of those wild guys who couldn't get his act together—he had been passionate about his career and was a huge success. *Shouldn't that be enough?* I thought, thinking about how much time I'd spent within Crawford's walls, throwing myself into every service. *Isn't that supposed to be enough?* It

scared me to think that we could spend so much time en-
grossed in our work, we might forget to ask ourselves, "Is
this really making me happy?"

I didn't go to Sam's funeral. I said good-bye there, in the
prep room, where Bill had combed Sam's hair and made his
cheeks pink again. Once Sam was dressed in the white suit
his family sent over and placed in the casket, all that was left
for me to do was double-check that Sam's clothing, hair, and
makeup were just as they were supposed to be—no mis-
takes. And so I gave the guys the go-ahead to get the shipping container, load it into the back of a hearse, and drive it
to the airport, where it was marked as cargo. In California,
staffers from another funeral home picked it up, and later
on, photos of the service were all over the Internet. The photographers found a way to focus in on Sam's famous friends,
as well as his gorgeous girlfriend, who stood crying as she
watched his casket lowered into the ground. It was a tragedy,
and I couldn't help but think that there was something very
unnatural about a young person dying.

What I didn't know then was that Sam wouldn't be the
last good-bye to come too soon.

BILL CALLED ME on my day off, and while Crawford
could be crazy, it was highly unusual for anyone on staff to call
my cell when I wasn't working. (Clients were a whole other
story, although I didn't mind those calls.) At first, I wasn't

going to answer it; I was about to meet up with a big group of high school friends, and work drama was the last thing I felt like dealing with. These dinners only happened a few times a year when people were in town, either moving back for good after "taking a year off to travel," or visiting from London or Los Angeles, two cities that Manhattan-raised "kids" liked to dabble in. (They always returned saying how it had been fun and all, but the city—whichever city it was—well, *it was no New York*.) But on the fifth ring, my curiosity got the better of me, and I picked up.

"Hello?" I said, looking in the mirror at my outfit. I had picked out a pair of black jeans and a leather Herve Leger jacket. *Now for the shoes*, I thought absentmindedly.

"Liz, it's Bill. Look, I know you're not on tonight, but do you think you could come in for an hour? A body just came in, and Monica and Tony are already gone, and I can't be upstairs *and* in the prep room at once."

I looked at my watch. It was already a quarter to eight and I was scheduled to meet my friends for dinner at nine all the way downtown at Locanda Verde. "This really isn't a good time," I said. Then I paused. Bill *never* called me outside of work. I don't even think I had given him my cell phone number—he must have gotten it from Tony's office. "Bill, is everything okay?"

Bill sighed into the phone. "Yeah, yeah, it's fine. I could just use a little help, and you're the only person who could get here quickly."

Technically, I wasn't allowed to work extra hours. With money being so tight, Crawford had cut back on overtime; they didn't even want us in the building after we had done our forty hours for the week. But Bill sounded exhausted, and he was right in that I was the only person who wasn't an hour's subway ride away. Plus, nobody else would be there to keep tabs on my hours—not like I was looking to collect.

If I wear flats, I can run over there and still have time to cab it downtown, I thought. "I'll be there in five minutes," I said.

When I got to Crawford, it felt darker and quieter than usual—much different than during the day, when staffers, florists, priests, rabbis, grieving widows, happy widows, men in Hermès loafers, women carrying fluffy dogs in their purses, and about a gazillion other people roamed through the halls. I could hear the Ramones coming from the prep room where Bill was working, probably on the new body that had been brought in. It was mostly covered in a white sheet. The only parts that were exposed were the face (which Bill was hunched over, trying to find a vein near the collarbone), and the hands, which were outside of the blanket at his sides, almost like in the yoga pose *Shavasana*. ("*Shavasana*" actually comes from two Sanskrit words meaning "corpse" and "posture." It's *literally* the death pose in yoga—something my Bikram instructor loved reminding me of.)

That's when his hands caught my eyes. Young hands. I stared at the fingertips. His nails were perfect—almost manicured. My gaze then went immediately up his arms to his head. My heart started to race. *Who was this person?* Somehow, for the first time, it dawned on me that I might know the guy on Bill's table.

And then Bill stood up, revealing the body's face.

I covered my mouth with my fingers, in shock. My legs became weak, and I felt a tingle in my jaw—a familiar sensation, something I usually felt when I was about to pass out. The next thing I knew I was on the floor, with Bill holding up my torso like I was a dead body.

"Liz?" he said, sounding genuinely worried.

My whole body shook against the cold tiles; my skin was cold and clammy. For another couple of minutes, I couldn't say anything. I had seen so many corpses at Crawford, but this time, the person on the table was someone I was supposed to be having dinner with in just a few minutes.

"It's Henry," I finally said, wiping tears and snot from my face. I was bright red, and my hands were shaking. "We went to school together."

Bill quickly covered the whole body with a sheet and put his arms around me. "I'm so sorry," he said. "I didn't know."

The truth is, none of us did—at least none of the twelve people I was supposed to have dinner with that night. To be fair, Henry and I weren't that close. I mostly knew him through other friends, and so our interactions over the years consisted mainly of clinking our glasses together or dancing in a big group of people. But the group of us had been texting and e-mailing for over a week to set up plans, and I knew I had seen Henry reply that he would be there. I pictured our friends—mostly Upper East Siders who had known each other since elementary school—sitting down at the table and sending increasingly offensive texts to Henry, probably accusing him of ditching them for a hot girl. We had been planning a big night: dinner and drinks first, then clubbing and an after-party on Gaby's rooftop. It all seemed so trivial now.

"Can I see the folder?" I asked Bill, who was standing in front of me with his arms crossed, a concerned look on his face. It was dead quiet, except for the sound of my sniffling. Somewhere in the middle of my breakdown, Bill had turned off the music.

"I need to see the folder," I said firmly.

Bill walked over to a shelf and handed it to me. I was looking for a death certificate. Sure enough, the cause of death was just what I had feared: drug overdose. And yet the word "overdose" flashed in front of my eyes, over and over, as if it might alter into something else if I just kept looking at it long enough. Like plenty of Manhattan prep school kids, Henry had experimented with drugs in high school. It was the usual stuff. Pot. Cocaine. Ecstasy. Nothing that you couldn't find at any party, on any Saturday night. He went off to a good college, and while we heard through the grapevine that his "experimenting" had turned into more of a full-on habit, nobody worried about it too much. College, we assumed, was for partying. We thought, *Okay, he's doing drugs. So what?* Who *hadn't* seen someone snort coke off a coffee table to get the night going or to push through a long night of studying?

Henry tried to get clean after graduation. At our little dinner reunion a year earlier, he looked better than he had in years: the skin under his eyes had lost that gray tint, and he had put on some healthy weight—a good twenty pounds. Instead of talking about it as a recovery—which, come on, that's what it was—people just said that Henry was "growing up, thank goodness." As though all the drugs and addiction weren't serious problems, but merely a silly hurdle he had been tripping over and finally cleared. *Bravo, Henry!* was the general tone.

I had heard he was using again, and while it bummed me out, I wasn't surprised. The Facebook photos said enough. Henry at a club with wide, red eyes. Henry with two girls on his lap at a club with four $500 bottles of vodka on the table, the empty ones turned over in an ice bucket. Henry looking thinner, and grayer, and unhappy. He may have been spoiled his whole life, but he was always a good time. And so for the most part, we ignored the mounting evidence that he was spiraling into addiction. *I'm sure if it were really bad, his close friends would do something*, I had thought the last time I bumped into Henry at a club. I shouldn't have trusted that they would.

"Who brought the body in?" I asked.

Bill explained that it had been the usual: the family called saying that the body was being brought in from the morgue. Henry had died early that morning, alone, in his bedroom. They wanted to keep things quiet. Didn't want a big scene, given the way Henry had died. That was all Bill knew.

I had to get out of that room. I thought about going home and calling Henry's mom, but something about it didn't feel right. I didn't know her very well, and I couldn't even imagine what she was going through. My dad's death had been painful, but I had had years to prepare for it. I also had the comfort of knowing that he had lived for sixty amazing years, filled with a loving marriage, fulfilling career, and kids who adored him. What would Henry's legacy be? What were *his* parents left with? Plus, Henry's mom had asked for privacy. Maybe she needed the night to herself before she could face the rest of Manhattan.

I found myself out on the sidewalk, a breeze whipping across my face, which was sticky with dried tears. Instinctively, I held my hand out for a cab, and as soon as one pulled up to the curb, I got in. "Greenwich and North Moore Streets," I said. Then I grabbed my phone and texted Gaby: ON MY WAY. I thought about adding, I HAVE BAD NEWS, or I HAVE TO TELL YOU ALL SOMETHING, but it was pointless. There was nothing I could write that would prepare them for the fact that Henry was not coming to dinner, because Henry was under a sheet, on a cold metal table, dead.

In the back of the cab, I took a few deep breaths and tried to get the image of Henry out of my mind. I had to get myself in a calm place so that I could be there for my friends. I was around death all the time—it was always hard, but it also wasn't shocking. For them, this would be a major blow—and maybe, for some, a wake-up call.

"Lizzie!" Gaby said when I arrived, jumping up from her seat and throwing her arms around me.

"Hi, guys," I said, forcing a smile. Three bottles of wine were already open on the table.

"We thought you ditched us," said Oliver, another childhood friend who lived a few blocks over from my mom's apartment.

I knew the longer I drew things out, the worse it would be. *Deep breath*, I told myself, holding on to the back of one of the chairs.

"I just came from Crawford," I said.

"I hope you washed your hands," joked Oliver, shouting from the side of the table.

"Guys, the thing is . . . um . . . it's Henry. Henry died of a drug overdose. This morning," I said.

The whole table went silent. I noticed a couple at the table on my right, probably out celebrating an anniversary or something, looking up at me in horror. *Well, you sure picked the wrong spot for a romantic evening*, I thought.

"Wait, *what?*" said Gaby, her face squishing into that expression people make before they cry. I grabbed a small bag of tissues from my bag, wishing I had more on hand. "Like, *Henry* Henry?"

Oliver looked down at the table, shaking his head. "Dude had been using some serious drugs for a while now," he said. "Should have just stuck with coke. Nobody fucking dies from blow."

A few other people were crying, and a cloud of grief hung over the table, somewhere above the plates of prosciutto and cheese. I thought about ways that I helped families when they came into Crawford, right after someone had died. If they were having a hard time, usually I would ask them to tell me a story about their loved one, like a favorite memory, or the funniest moment they ever shared. *That could work here*, I thought.

"Is it completely hypocritical or totally appropriate to order another couple bottles of wine and toast in Henry's honor?" I said. "Not sure if it will be a toast or a roast, but there will be some good stories."

"I like that idea," said Jen, the old classmate who had hugged me at my father's funeral. Jen had dated Henry's brother for a while—she knew him better than the rest of us. "Henry would have liked it, too."

For the next five hours, we talked about the time Henry crashed his dad's brand-new Bentley, the crazy parties he used to throw at his parents' beach house, his affinity for

Asians and blondes (he wouldn't date anyone outside of those categories). Nobody had lived the life of a privileged WASP better than Henry, and even though he was a woman-izer who often had white powder around the edges of his nose, everybody liked him. (Well, everyone who wasn't sleeping with him liked him; he made any girl who was actu-ally interested in him batshit crazy.) He was sweet and funny when he wasn't strung out on whatever pill or powder was hidden in his pocket. And love him or hate him, he had been one of us, a neighborhood kid, who got caught up in the same crap many of us had tried at some point or another. We all knew it could have been anyone at the table. This time, it was Henry.

I couldn't sleep that night, and when my eyes were still wide open at six a.m., I called the only person who I knew for sure would be awake: my mom. She had never been much of a sleeper; even when Dad was alive, she was the first one awake in the mornings, two cups of Earl Grey deep before the rest of us had climbed out of bed. I knew she would find out about Henry eventually, anyway—news had a habit of traveling fast up and down Fifth Avenue, like a game of tele-phone played from penthouse to penthouse instead of ear to ear. By the time the story of Henry's death came out the other end, who knew what people would have done with it.

Mom picked up on the first ring.

"Hello, Mom?" I said, not realizing I was crying until I opened my mouth. I looked around my empty bedroom and suddenly wished so desperately that it was ten years earlier. Henry would have been alive. Dad would have been alive. Whole families that had been broken into pieces would suddenly have been reglued.

"Elizabeth? Are you all right?" said Mom, sounding concerned.

I wanted to tell her about Henry, but all that was coming out of me was a puddle of emotion that had been pent up too long. Mom asked again if I was okay, and I realized I must be freaking her out. *Say something,* I told myself, trying to catch my breath. I opened my mouth to explain. Instead, all that came out was, "I . . . [sniffle] . . . miss . . . [sniffle] . . . Dad."

"You've been stabbed!" Mom said, now yelling into the phone in a panic. *"Where are you? Who stabbed you?"*

I was still sobbing. "No, no, no," I said. *"Dad.* I said I miss *Dad.*"

"Oh my God, you gave me a heart attack," she said, audibly relieved. We were both silent for a moment, and then, in the strong, calm tone only she was able to pull off in hard moments, she said, "Elizabeth, everything is going to be okay. Take a deep breath."

I inhaled and let it out right into the receiver.

"Now tell me what's wrong," she said.

I rehashed the whole night, from Bill's call to seeing Henry there under a sheet—his hands, white, probably cold (I hadn't touched them). I told her about the dinner and my friends, and how it seemed that life was going really fast all of a sudden, and I didn't know how to slow it down. When you're young, it feels like life is really long—and there are so many possibilities, it's almost overwhelming to think about all that you can do. But all around me, things were ending. At work, with my friends, even the way the family felt now, with Dad gone. So many things were just . . . over. Henry might have been young and fun and privileged, but none of that was bringing him back.

"Do you want me to come to the funeral?" said Mom softly.

I shook my head no, even though she couldn't see me. I didn't want to put her through seeing Henry in a casket. She hadn't known him, but she knew *of* him, and it seemed like a lot of unnecessary sadness to put her through. She deserved a break from the bad stuff in life. "No, you don't have to do that," I said, wiping tears from my face. "I'll probably be running around anyway. You wouldn't even see me."

I expected her to protest a *little*, but Mom simply said, "Okay," and told me that if I still couldn't sleep, I should take a walk—it always worked for her. It wasn't until we hung up the phone that I wished, maybe for the first time since Dad died, that I was back in their apartment. It seemed weird to think that Mom was still there, eating at the same dining room table, reading on the same sofa, walking by the same fireplace in the living room where we used to open presents Christmas morning. Everyone else had moved away and moved on. I thought about dialing her number again and asking her to walk with me but talked myself out of it. *I can handle this alone*, I thought.

"ARE WE BURNING or burying?" asked one of the Crawford staffers, some part-time guy from our sister funeral home who was helping out a few days a week.

"Seriously, could you not?" I said, shaking my head. *What an asshole.* "This is someone's son. And we're burying, thank you."

I wasn't personally working on Henry's funeral, but I couldn't help but check in on what Tony was doing to make sure that everything was just right. A lot of people I knew would be there, and I didn't want any missteps. Bill was already finished working on the body, so all that was left was to check that the photo boards had been placed in optimal positions around the room so that they wouldn't interfere with the receiving line, and that the projection screen was working so the family could play the photo slideshow of Henry's life. Tony said that not *once* during the planning did Henry's parents talk about the fact that he died of an overdose—instead they decided to show pictures of him sailing, skiing, and surfing—even though most of them were from before high school (and before he got into drugs). "We want this to be a celebration," they said. Normally I would have agreed with them, although it was hard to feel the same about Henry's death as I did about older clients. Henry had had every opportunity—a few *too* many, perhaps—and there was something tragic about how he wasted them.

There was a line out the door ten minutes into the service. It was open casket, and since Henry didn't die in, say, a terrible car wreck that damaged his face, like many of the other younger deaths I'd seen, he looked like he was just nursing a hangover from the night before. It was hard to be at Crawford and *not* be working. I tried my best not to mill about the room like one of those robotic vacuum cleaners, picking things up and cleaning things off. I even wore my black blazer, something I'd normally never wear to a funeral as a guest.

Henry's parents were the first to enter. They walked slowly up to the casket, which was normal. Seeing a loved one laid out was so final, most families approached it like tiptoeing up to the edge of a cliff, and then—with one look down—jumping. I stood in the hall where Tony was lingering and saw him tear up as Henry's mom took a look at her son and held on to the casket, crying, "No." Her husband tried to fight back his own tears while simultaneously holding her up. It wasn't just sad, it was heart wrenching. And even though Tony had seen thousands of services, I knew why he was crying. The fact was, it didn't need to be this way. Henry could still be here. I thought of my friends who still did drugs—sometimes bending down to "tie their shoe," only to open a small plastic vial and snort coke off their door key—and wished, for them, that they could witness this moment. *Who could do this to their parents, if they knew that this is what it would be like?* I thought.

Then it hit me: Was I really much different? I had been alienating my mom since Dad died. She had even offered to come tonight—a big gesture for a woman who almost collapsed in her Manolos when I told her I was working at a funeral home—and I had shut her down. I looked over again at Henry's mom, who kept smoothing out the lapel on her son's blazer. (It was already wrinkle-free; Bill had made sure of it.) *Have I been doing this to my mom?* I thought. *Does she feel this alone?* There was nothing Henry could do to take his mother's grief away, but I was very much alive. I reached for my phone to call my mom and tell her that I'd changed my mind, I did want her there— but she didn't pick up. My heart sank.

Once Henry's father gave the okay, Tony called down to Monica to open the door and begin ushering in visitors. There were whispers in the foyer: "Did you hear? I think it was an overdose," or, "It wasn't an overdose, he just got a bad batch," but *nobody* said a word about how Henry died once they were in the viewing room. The early arrivals were mostly friends of Henry's parents and neighbors, but after a half hour or so, my friends started coming. "It's so fucking weird to see you here," said Oliver. "I can't believe you work in this place." I just pointed to the stairs. "Up the steps to your right. I'll see you in there."

Oliver started to walk and then turned to face me. "At least Henry would be happy to have a cute girl helping out with his funeral."

Pretty soon, I started to notice a, uh, *theme*, you might say. The line entering the foyer became less and less women in pearl earrings and men in custom-tailored suits, and more and more tall blondes in fitted black dresses, and young Asian women in heels a *little* too high for the occasion. At first there were ten or so, then twenty, then thirty. It was like every girl Henry had ever taken back to his posh bachelor pad was there to ask why he had never called her back. At least now he finally had a good excuse.

"This is pretty crazy," I whispered to Oliver, who was standing in the back of the room against the wall. "You're going to die when you see all these girls working their way up the stairs."

"Bottle whores?" he said, his voice quivering. He was trying to crack a smile, but I could tell that the wake was getting to him. Grief could be like that. Some people were able to hold off the pain of losing someone, like Oliver had done at dinner, but only for so long. Eventually it would catch up with them. "Shame this place doesn't allow drinks. I could really use one right now," he said.

I handed Oliver a tissue from the pack I carried around and rubbed his back. "I know it's hard," I said.

He wiped his eyes and then used the tissue to blow his nose, almost playing it off like he had a cold. "It's just weird," he said. "We knew the guy for twenty years. He had the perfect life, like, he had *everything*."

I realized then that Oliver wasn't necessarily crying for Henry, but for himself. Oliver had certainly done his share of drugs, and anyone could accidentally OD. Seeing Henry there in the casket, it was our own mortality staring all of us in the face. With one stupid decision, this fairy tale of a life we'd been born into could be gone.

"I've got to get my shit together," said Oliver, straightening his collar and stuffing the tissue into the inside pocket of his blazer. He looked around the room one more time, mostly focusing on the casket, which was surrounded by flowers and people walking with their heads down. "I know I already asked this, but seriously, how do you work here?"

Then he kissed me on the cheek, slipped down the stairs, and left.

I stayed until the end. As weird as Crawford may have felt to Oliver, it had become a second home to me. This wasn't a total coincidence—funeral homes were initially designed to look like just that, *homes*. And the fancy décor at Crawford felt familiar, not just to me, but I'm sure to many Manhattanites who'd grown up in prewar buildings with carved moldings and velvet couches. Maybe it was from all the long hours I'd spent there, or the fact that it was the place I'd said good-bye to my dad, but Crawford gave me a strange comfort. And even though I wasn't obligated to stay at Henry's service, I wanted to be there, in the background, just in case Tony needed an extra hand refilling the water or getting the projector to work. The service ran smoothly, though, and after two hours, most guests had already made their way out the door and back to their wonderful lives at their wonderful apartments. I remembered that from Dad's funeral—how bizarre it was that we were all in this one space, grieving together, but how afterward, Mom, Max, and I would go home and things would never be the same. Everyone was secretly happy they weren't us, at least in that moment. And now I felt that way for Henry's parents, who were lingering near the casket, knowing it was time to go but not wanting to leave their son there, alone and dead.

Tony let them stay almost a full half hour past their scheduled service time, even though it would mean he would get home to his own family a bit later. I walked down to the foyer, picking up all the random things that fall out of people's pockets and purses—change, mass cards, the clear wrappers from the mints I'd put in bowls around the building. I thought of Henry's parents, still upstairs, and realized that I didn't just miss my dad . . . I missed my mom, too. I pulled out my phone again and called her, but still no answer. *You always pick up*, I thought, getting a little nervous. *Maybe she's out to dinner?*

"I'm heading out," I said to Monica, who looked half-asleep leaning up against the reception desk. *Yeah, because you did so much tonight*, I thought, rolling my eyes. Without looking at me, she raised one hand and motioned like she was shooing me out the door. I looked at my phone once more to see if my mom had called back, but she hadn't. Disappointed, I grabbed my purse and walked out into the night air.

When I stepped out onto the sidewalk and looked up, there was Mom, wearing one of Dad's oversized sweaters and a pair of stretch pants. She was standing outside Crawford with Maggie, clutching her leash. It was as if she knew I finally needed her . . . that all the walls I had put up after Dad died were crumbling down, and I didn't want to be left standing in the ruins, alone.

"You came," I said, a ball of happiness and relief lodged in my throat.

"You're my daughter," said Mom, holding out her arm to hug me. "And I know when my daughter needs me." Maggie panted at our feet, as if to remind us that she, too, was partaking in the moment.

"I'm so sorry," I said, falling into her arms. Instead of wiping my tears, I pushed my face into Dad's sweater.

Mom pulled me in close and squeezed me. "I'm sorry, too. How about some Entenmann's crumb cake?" she said. "I have one at home."

I laughed. My mom's mom had been a big fan of the grocery-store crumb cakes ever since she was a little girl. They would eat them on the weekends for breakfast, or when company stopped by for coffee. After Gram, my maternal grandma, died, my mom would buy an Entenmann's on days when she missed her and needed a little piece of comfort. We never actually ate the cake part (that went to Maggie); we just picked off the buttery crumbs dusted in powdered sugar and nibbled on them in between sips of tea. I hadn't eaten one in years, but in that moment, there was nothing I wanted to do more.

"Yes, please," I said, taking Maggie's red leather leash from my mom's grip. It was just then that I looked down at Mom's feet. "Um, are those . . . Aerosoles?"

She looked down, too, and kicked up her left foot, like she was posing in a fashion ad. "They are!" she said, smiling. "You were right—they're the most comfortable things ever."

I laughed even harder. And with that, we both took a step forward, together, toward home.

TWELVE

A Scandal

S hit really started to hit the fan at Crawford after the Goldstein funeral. Monica and her posse of RWHMs (receptionists who hated me) and a few funeral directors had been clawing their way under my skin for months. It was like they couldn't wait to dig their square acrylic nails into everything I did and said. The only thing keeping me sane was knowing that I was good at my job and that Tony relied on me. We had gotten to a point where he could just nod at me from across a room, and I would instinctively know what the issue was and how to fix it. A crying mistress, a drunk brother, an uninvited sibling—I could handle it all quickly and professionally. Which is the precise reason why Mrs. Goldstein requested that I be on the floor for her husband's funeral.

One of the newer staffers, a former part-time guy named

Derek, was supposed to handle the funeral. But Mrs. Goldstein didn't like that he smelled like smoke from his hourly cigarette breaks out back, and she was outright offended by the way he hung around the front desk, talking to Monica and the other receptionists. (Derek was an easy recruit to Monica's little Crawford clique.) "I don't see anyone working," Mrs. Goldstein said under her breath as I happened to walk by her on my way to my office.

I turned around and put my hand gently on her arm. "Can I help you with something, Mrs. Goldstein?" I asked. I knew her name because there were only a few services that week, and I had already read through all the folders. Also, the Goldsteins were a prominent Manhattan family. I had seen the late Mr. Goldstein and his children (both in their fifties), and *their* children, at charity galas over the years. Mrs. Goldstein didn't know me, but I knew her, and that was all that mattered now.

She immediately looked relieved. "I'm not impressed by the man handling my husband's funeral," she said. "I expected better treatment than this."

I introduced myself, invited Mrs. Goldstein into my office, and handed her a cup of ice water. She was an important client, and I knew that Tony would be upset if she was displeased with her experience with us. Derek *had* taken care of most of the details—the casket had been delivered, Bill had already prepped the body, and there was a full guest list. But Mrs. Goldstein was what she was: a wealthy, slightly snotty woman who wanted her guests to be greeted in the manner to which they were accustomed. A guy in a threadbare suit who smelled like a pack of Marlboros, and a gum-snapping receptionist who led visitors to the viewing room by pointing to the elevator? Not exactly what she had in mind.

I knew I would have to run it by Tony, so I asked Mrs. Goldstein to wait a moment while I spoke with him. It took just two minutes of explaining the situation for Tony to say I should stay with Mrs. Goldstein. We had *another* high-profile service that night, and he would be busy with that. Splitting us up to handle both clients made perfect sense, and I was the only one who would recognize the non-celebrity VIPs as they came in anyway. "I'll tell Derek," he said to me. "I don't want anybody on that floor but you."

It took less than half an hour for word to spread through Crawford. Derek was pissed. Monica was chirping away so fast, her head was in danger of exploding. I was accustomed to the side eye and snide comments, but the harassment was now way past subtle. "Only Tony's princess is allowed on the floor," Monica said, in English this time, as I walked toward the bathroom. "Tony wants her *all* to himself, I guess," said Derek, fully sucked into the drama.

I felt shaky rage boiling up in me. "The only reason that I'm working this funeral is because the client specifically requested *not* to work with you," I said, glaring at Derek.

Monica mumbled something else, and the receptionist next to her laughed.

"What?" I said. "What is it? If you're going to talk about me, at least do it in English so I can understand you."

"Fine," said Monica, a smug look on her face, like she was enjoying this. "I was saying that maybe if he was having an affair with the boss too, that might also help him 'do his job' or whatever you want to call it."

"That's it," I said. "I've had it. I'm going to complain to management and the union about you. You can't just go around spreading insane rumors about people."

"Don't you know the rule?" said Monica, still smiling. "There's a five-thousand-dollar fine for complaining about union members. We don't tell on each other."

I'd happily spend that just to piss you off, I thought to myself.

What Monica and company didn't understand was that the better you are at your job, the more the boss trusts you. Tony knew I would impress his top clients, just like he knew that he could ask me to call the Carlyle, an expensive hotel Crawford partnered with, and I'd work with the hostess of the restaurant to set up a repast—no problem. It was seamless, not because I was sleeping with the guy, but because I treated every client like they were a family friend or a neighbor. And in a lot of cases, they were.

Just before the Goldstein service, Tony called me into his office to tell me that he would be tied up all night with funeral *numero dos* and that I shouldn't bother him under any circumstances. "Whatever it is, just handle it," he told me. I had already spent the past two hours refilling tissue boxes, memorizing the guest list, picking rose petals off the carpet, and arranging a car to pick Mrs. Goldstein up so that she had one less thing to think about.

The service itself went as planned. I ushered guests from the hallway to the viewing room but never lingered. I knew the golden rule of any private affair: you never want to see the person running things behind the scenes. She should be invisible, and all the client should see is a perfectly run event. When older guests got off the elevator, I escorted them into the viewing room and then immediately rushed back to help the next group.

"Elizabeth, is that *you?*" one woman whispered to me after stepping off the lift into the hallway. I recognized her from Elaine's.

"Nice to see you, Mrs. Watters," I said.

"I heard you had been working here but I thought it couldn't possibly be true," she said.

I forced a smile. "Wonders never cease," I said, and pointed her toward the room where Mr. Goldstein was laid out (in a tuxedo, of course).

It wasn't until most guests were gone that I found Mrs. Goldstein sitting by herself in the back of the viewing room. She looked confused, and so even though I had been keeping to myself most of the night, I went over to her and crouched down by her side. "Is there anything you need, Mrs. Goldstein?" I said.

She looked to her left and right, then leaned toward my ear. "What's a *shomer*?" she whispered.

The Goldsteins were benefactors to one of the most popular synagogues in the city, but they weren't, it turned out, particularly religious. Apparently, several of the guests had asked her when the *shomer* was coming, and to her horror, Mrs. Goldstein had no idea what they were talking about. I explained gently that a *shomer* was someone who, in Jewish tradition, watched the body overnight before the burial.

"Is it expensive?" Mrs. Goldstein asked.

"Not really, less than twenty dollars an hour," I said, looking at my watch. It was nine o'clock at night, and the staff would be back in ten hours. "It'll cost about two hundred bucks," I said.

"Oh, well then of course, get me a *shomer*," she said.

Tony was still held up with the other funeral, and I would need a union funeral director to actually hire one. (It was a weird loophole, but since my title wasn't recognized by the union, I had to have union staffers do certain tasks.) Since Derek had been scheduled to work that night anyway, he was the only one around. Well, he and Monica, who was twirling her hair around her fingernail and trying to sneak texts under the desk. Pretty much the last thing a client wanted to see was a staffer LOL-ing with a friend while he or she waited for service.

"Derek, I need you to please call up a *shomer*," I said.

The company we used—yes, a *shomer* company (I know, so crazy)—closed at ten p.m., so we didn't have much time.

"No can do," said Derek. "You need Tony to do that. But that should be no problem for you."

"Tony put me in charge of this funeral, and he's busy with another client tonight," I said. "He would want this to happen. Please make the order."

"Don't do it," said Monica, looking at Derek. "It wasn't in the contract. Who's going to pay for that shit if this woman bails on the bill?"

"That's easy," I said, about to burst. "I'll pay for it. It's two hundred dollars, for Christ's sake! Now please make the call."

Derek moved both his hands behind his back, as if he were in handcuffs. "My hands are tied," he said, stifling laughter.

There was only one thing left to do: I had to get Tony. I was mad at myself for not being able to handle the whole night on my own, as I knew Tony expected. But I was furious with Derek and Monica. The whole "Tony's princess" routine was getting old—*real* old—and now their antics were keeping me from doing my job. I walked upstairs and saw Tony standing outside his office, looking at the client's bill, most likely making sure that they had provided everything the client paid for; the company was in no position to lose money due to a silly oversight.

"Hey, uh, Tony?" I said, walking up awkwardly behind him. "I have to ask you for something."

He whirled around, took one look at me, and crinkled up his forehead. It was his *I'm pissed* look, and I hated that it was directed at me. "I thought I told you not to interrupt me tonight," he said.

I told him what happened. I knew I sounded like a snitch, but I didn't care. It was now half past nine, and I needed someone to make the call for a *shomer*. Tony brushed past me and barreled down the stairs, straight toward the reception desk. Derek and Monica didn't even have time to put their cell phones away before Tony pulled both of them into the back room and went off. I mean, the man flew off the handle. "Are you fucking kidding me with this bullshit?" he said, turning bright red. "A phone call? You fucking people can't make a phone call for a client who's shelling out eighty grand for a funeral here?"

Derek looked down during the whole tirade, but Monica's eyes were focused on me. I could have felt vindicated—Tony clearly had my back, and there was nothing they could do or say to change that. But mostly, I felt defeated. This type of drama wasn't what I had signed up for. We worked in the death business, for God's sake. Every single day, we saw people on one of the worst days of their lives. We saw people grieving their kids, their parents, their friends. What was so bad about our lives that we couldn't even act civilly toward each other?

Typically, if Tony got mad, he was over it before the next

shift. But this time, things were different. Two days after the *shomer* incident (yes, we hired one, just in the nick of time), Tony called me into his office. I figured he was going to reprimand me for not handling the situation myself, but instead he sat calmly at his desk, rubbing his forehead. He looked physically ill.

"Someone called my wife," he said.

I raised my eyebrows. Tony's wife called Crawford all the time; I wasn't sure why anyone would call her, but there could be a gazillion reasons. "Okay," I said, looking for more information.

"Someone called my wife and told her that you and I are having an affair."

If my jaw weren't hinged, it would have dropped right to the floor. There was no way Monica was *that* evil. I mean maybe, *maybe* there was a chance. I thought of Tony's outburst in the back room and the way she had stared at me, and chills ran up my back.

"That's . . . that's just ridiculous," I said, still in disbelief. "She doesn't believe them, does she? She has to know that these people are out of their minds."

"I told her that, and she says, 'Okay, if you say so,'" said Tony. "But she's barely speaking to me. I don't blame her, either. It's a violation. These fucking people, they have no boundaries."

I offered to take a vacation. Max and his friends were planning a trip to Laos and Thailand; I could tag along with them for a few weeks. A little space might do the situation good—you know, let it breathe a little. Air out the drama. I hadn't taken a real vacation in what felt like forever. Just as my mind landed somewhere on top of an elephant, sauntering along a river, Tony pulled me out of it.

"No," he said. "You aren't the problem here. We need to report this."

We scheduled a meeting with the president of Crawford, who was normally not someone we dealt with on a day-today basis. He had, however, approved my title change, my schedule, and my office—he even helped us get around the union rules to make it all happen. Tony and I assumed that he'd be on our side, but rumor about the affair had traveled so far through the company, it had found its way to the president's desk. "You two *do* spend a lot of time together," he said. When Tony protested—I was too shocked to say anything—we were told that it was an HR issue, and so . . . off we went to HR.

Crawford had been a family business for generations, but it was now owned by a parent company that dealt with a whole bunch of funeral homes in the area. Of course, nobody at Crawford wanted the clients to know that; they came to us because Crawford felt exclusive. Nobody wanted to have their wake at the Olive Garden of funeral homes, especially Manhattan's social elite. Crawford was still run like a family business, at least on the inside—but any major HR issues were dealt with on a higher level. And so Tony and I went to corporate headquarters in Bayonne, New Jersey, to meet with the HR manager, a friendly woman named Pattie, who just about spat out her coffee when we explained what we were being accused of by Monica and some of the other staffers.

"You're pulling my leg," she said, fully amused. "The two of you? An affair? *Ha!*"

Tony and I nodded in agreement. Even he knew it was ridiculous. The guys I went out with were twenty years younger, ten times richer, and a hundred times more attractive. Not that those were requirements or anything, but that was just reality; an overweight, graying family man was hardly the guy I was trying to bag. Mom had suffered enough already. Elaine would have up and died. I might have been the rebel in the family, but I wasn't a freaking masochist.

"So what do we do about this?" said Tony. "They're saying they've seen us out to dinner together, that they 'know' this is happening. It's out of control."

Pattie still couldn't get over it. "An affair, I swear, I've heard it all," she said, still smiling. "In your dreams, Tony!"

"Okay, okay, we get it, it's ridiculous," said Tony. But when he went on to say that the staff had called his wife— and that as a result, he had tensions at work *and* at home— Pattie became more serious. I added that I was starting to feel like I couldn't work there anymore; Monica was straight-up harassing me, and I was awake at night with anxiety thinking about what she would say about me next. The notion that Tony and I were sleeping together was laughable, but the situation itself was anything but funny.

Pattie's instructions were twofold: For starters, Tony and I were to spend less time together. "Just until this dies down," she said. From there on out, we were only to converse when absolutely necessary and would need to work on separate funerals. I would have to go back to a normal schedule, meaning no more Monday through Friday, which had been approved months before by both Tony and the president of Crawford. It actually had nothing to do with playing favorites; the simple fact was, when I worked with a family on a service, they expected me to be *at* that service. And since my days off had been Tuesday and Friday, and Upper East Side clients usually wanted to plan funerals for weekdays before their friends left for their weekend country homes, it was impossible to guarantee I would be there without Crawford having to pay me overtime to come in. But all the staffers saw was that I had a nine-to-five, weekday-only schedule—something that was almost unheard of in the funeral business.

Pattie also said that I should talk to a therapist about my work stress. I scoffed at the idea; I hadn't even gone to therapy after my dad died, so the idea that I would go now over some bitchy coworker seemed crazy. But when Pattie wrote down the name of a therapist that took union insurance and said that she would call me the next day to confirm that I had made an appointment, I knew it was less of a "suggestion" and more of a requirement. Crawford had to cover its ass, and apparently that required examining my head.

In a stroke of luck, the therapist was actually just fifteen blocks from my apartment. Before my first session, I called my friend Ben for lunch. His hedge fund office was nearby, and he was able to scoot out of work to meet me at Café Boulud—his fancy suggestion—for a bite before I bared my soul to some poor woman in librarian glasses on a couch. (At least that's how I pictured it; like I said, I had never actually been to therapy before.) It would have been much more practical to meet for salads or sandwiches, but this was Ben, who did everything to the max—including lunch.

"What kind of therapist takes union insurance?" said Ben, chewing on a slice of bread. "Everyone knows the top doctors in this city don't bother with *any* insurance."

"I don't know," I said. "The payment plan is the least of my problems."

Ben called the waiter over and ordered a bottle of viognier, with two glasses. I told him I couldn't drink—going into my first therapy session with a buzz hardly seemed like the most amazing idea. But Ben insisted it would shake off my nerves and instructed the waiter to pour me a "healthy serving" to go with my salad.

"Drink," he said, raising his glass to his lips and instructing me to do the same.

"I can't," I said. "This is serious."

Ben rolled his eyes. "Liz, there is *nothing* serious about

this. It's a fucking joke. Do they really think you're going to sleep your way to the *top of a funeral home?*"

"I know it sounds crazy," I said. "But that's the situation."

"Bullshit. You're not even sleeping with me. If you're not sleeping with me, you're sure as hell not sleeping with *that* guy."

I chuckled and took a sip of the wine to appease Ben but didn't touch the rest of it. The truth was, my stomach was in knots. I wasn't super into the idea of spilling my guts to a total stranger, and I was worried she would judge me. It was too easy for people to label me as the spoiled rich girl—granted, I was lunching extravagantly on a weekday—and who was to say that this therapist, a union therapist, no less, would be any different? Ben spent the rest of lunch trying to get me to skip the appointment and drive out to the Hamptons with him on his new BMW motorcycle. I loved bikes, and I didn't mind the Hamptons, but that wasn't my life anymore. I wasn't the get-up-and-go girl I had been a couple of years before. This was my job. I had to see it through.

The therapist's office was on a beautiful tree-lined street, but the inside of the building itself was shabby. It looked more like apartments than offices, and I was surprised when I walked straight into the office rather than into a waiting area. "You must be Elizabeth," said the therapist, who simply went by Sue. (Not Dr. Sue, just . . . Sue. Although to be fair, she wasn't a doctor.) Sue was wearing a long skirt with a baggy cardigan, with her curly hair frizzed out all over the place. It was all very nineties chic, if, you know, the nineties had been chic.

The office wasn't much better. Bookshelves lined the walls; there was even a shelf in front of the one lonely window in the whole unit, blocking all the light. The wood floor creaked when I walked, despite the burgundy rug covering most of it. The blinds were plastic. The furniture didn't match. Everything smelled like dust. I immediately regretted not drinking more of the wine.

"Nice to meet you," I said, trying to decide where in this hellhole I would sit. Sue took care of it for me, motioning for me to take a seat on the couch, which was made of navy blue pleather.

"So you're having some trouble with the other staff members," Sue began.

I shrugged. "Yeah, you could say that." *How did I get roped into this again?*

"Why don't you take me to when the problems started and walk me through it. Does that sound like a plan?"

"You mean, my first day? I thought we only had forty-five minutes," I said.

"You've been having trouble since you started?" said Sue, writing something down in her notebook.

"Yup," I said, folding my hands in front of me.

"Give me the CliffsNotes, then," said Sue, flashing a warm smile.

I sighed loudly and started telling her what happened—
how Monica hated me from my first day, people stealing my
lunch, Tony giving me a promotion, the incident with the
shomer, the rumors about an affair. Sue was scribbling non-
stop, taking down notes and occasionally muttering, "Uh-
huh," or "Okay, got it . . ." After a full twenty minutes of
listening to me explain the situation, Sue took off her glasses,
rubbed her eyes, and set her notebook down on the small
side table next to her chair.

"Elizabeth, where do you live?" she asked. I suspected
she already knew the answer.

"On Fifth Avenue," I said.

"That's a pretty ring," she said, pointing to my sapphire.
"Do you wear that to work?"

"It was a gift from my parents," I said. "I wear it all the
time."

"And that watch?"

"Yes. It was my father's," I said, starting to get annoyed.
"But me living in a nice apartment, and having nice things,
does not make it okay for people to harass me at work and
make my life hell."

"You're absolutely right," said Sue. "It doesn't. But
you're the outsider in this situation. You don't speak their
language—figuratively *and*, in the case of this Monica
woman, literally."

"So how do I fix that?" I asked, feeling a little flustered.

Sue shook her head. "You don't. If they're getting to you

this badly, it might be time to look for something else. There's not much I can do to help you."

I didn't want to let Monica and her stupid friends win. In the world I grew up in, people didn't always get along perfectly, but they could put on a happy face for the sake of appearances. No matter where you went, you were bound to run into *someone* you didn't like. A party, a fund-raiser, the Met Ball—they were chock-full of people who hated each other's guts but knew how to kiss on both cheeks and move on. As Elaine used to say, "Friends close, enemies closer."

"That can't be the answer," I said. I didn't want to cry, not in front of this stranger. But the idea of giving up because of the way other people were behaving did not sit well with me.

Sue had stopped taking notes entirely and was now leaning forward in her chair, her elbows on her thighs. "Tell me if I have this right," she said. "You shop on Madison Avenue. You drink . . . I don't know . . . green juices for breakfast. You get weekly manicures. And that bag you're carrying . . . I bet it's not a fake."

Normally this kind of overgeneralization would offend me, but Sue was pretty spot-on. She also spoke in a kind way, like she was verbalizing something nobody else at Crawford ever would. I *was* different. I *was* an outsider. And while the middle-aged men in the business weren't threatened by me (they were mostly confused about why someone would ever *choose* to work funerals), Monica was a different story. It suddenly clicked: I was probably everything she hated about Manhattan women, all rolled into one. And not because I was a bad person, but because people—including Crawford clients—had been treating her like she was inferior for years.

"They're never going to understand you fully," said Sue. "And you need to realize that you don't understand them, either."

I nodded slowly. Sue was right. As much as I'd focused on how Monica and the rest of the staff had me all wrong, I didn't have a true sense of what their lives were like, either. Accepting defeat wasn't my strong suit, but I had a sense that I wasn't going to win this time. I thanked Sue for her time, and the two of us agreed that we didn't need to do any more sessions. For the time being, I would just keep my head down at work and stay away from Tony as much as possible . . . at least until things had eased up for him at home. Sue was pretty sure that all the drama would pass; eventually, Monica would find something else to gossip about. But none of that would happen if the staff felt like I was getting special treatment. They needed to see me doing more of the grunt work, and that would mean that I wouldn't be able to spend as much time with the clients— which was my *actual* job. I started to feel like I might be moving backward.

More than anything, I wished that I could call my dad. He would have known what to do. Mom, on the other hand,

THIRTEEN

This Job Is Killing Me

My father loved cheesy sayings. He was practically famous for them. One of his favorites was, "Choose a job you love, and you'll never work a day in your life." I know, I know, obviously Dad didn't invent this line—but he was an ardent repeater, and really *did* live his life that way. He left the apartment every morning in good spirits and returned home just the same. I never remember him staring at his phone or checking e-mails in off hours, either. On my fifteenth birthday, there was a disaster at the office—a major deal was on the verge of falling through. Dad didn't sweat it, though. For him, the bigger disaster would have been missing me blow out my candles.

I inherited many traits from my dad, but his ability to separate his work life from his personal life was not one of them. I loved my job when it came to helping clients plan services, but I was at the end of my rope with the staff. Between the affair drama, Tony's growing obsession with the bottom line, and the constant scrutiny of the union bosses, who now had their eyes on me, I could no longer do my job. Not the way I wanted to, anyway. Going to work in the morning started to feel like . . . well . . . *work*. I had always promised myself I'd never be one of those people you see walking around Manhattan like zombies, practically on a drip feed of Starbucks and who knows what else. I was friendly with plenty of people who bragged about how many hours they'd banked at the office that week, who wanted everyone to know they were "so busy" they could never put their phones away, not even during Thanksgiving dinner, or as one girlfriend of mine experienced, during sex. (If there were ever a good reason to leave a man with throbbing blue balls, that has got to be it.)

There was no getting around it: Crawford was wearing me down. Even the therapist told me there was no hope for things to get better. Tony had taken to avoiding me completely, making both of our jobs harder. Plus, I was back to shift work—late nights and early mornings that made it almost impossible for me to follow up with clients, since they came into Crawford during normal daytime hours. Even the clients seemed like they were changing. Maybe everyone was just in a funk because the economy was still in the tank, but as clients had tightened their Chanel purse strings, they'd also become somewhat . . . cranky. I'd been lucky; for most of my time at Crawford, clients had treated me respectfully, some even sending me thoughtful, handwritten thank-you notes after services. I'd never in my life had someone treat me like I was below them; suddenly, it was like I was a minion for pissed-off customers to dump their baggage on. It was an awful eye-opener, and I wondered if I was just getting a taste of what Monica had been dealing with for years.

The shift started with one family, the Whitmans, whom I had known from prep school. Mr. Whitman's son had been in my tennis classes back in elementary school. He and his sister were classic spoiled brats; they once refused to play tennis because their nanny had forgotten to pack their rackets and the club's rackets weren't their preferred brand. I'm talking about eight-year-olds, here.

Mr. Whitman had come in to plan his father's funeral. I greeted him warmly, the way I always greeted clients, but he barely even looked me in the eye, much less recognized me from all the summers my family had spent at tennis matches and charity parties with his. But it wasn't my job to remind him—and if he was anything like his son, I knew I'd want this over as quickly as possible. Mr. Whitman refused to sit down, meaning I had to stand as well to write down his requests for his father's services. He shouted out orders, almost like he was angry, although I wanted to give him the benefit of the doubt that it was just the grief talking. *Deep breaths*, I told myself, trying to keep my Italian temper at bay. What I really wanted to do was tell Mr. Whitman to take his dead father, and his attitude, elsewhere.

The service was standard. I didn't go out of my way like I normally did to make it special. Mr. Whitman didn't want my suggestions, and he certainly didn't want me pulling off any sweet surprises, which most clients loved. As I stood in the hallway, guiding the few visitors into the viewing room, I wondered if Mr. Whitman Senior had the same personality as his oh-so-charming son. That could explain the rows of empty chairs.

I poked my head into the viewing room—totally normal procedure—to make sure that everything was running smoothly. It looked fine, so I turned to walk back down the hall when I bumped into Mr. Whitman. "What are you doing here?" he shouted at me. I could feel my face burning up. *Breathe, Lizzie. Breathe.*

"I'm just checking in to make sure you have everything you need," I said. "Is there anything else I can do for you, Mr. Whitman?"

He looked at me with disgust. *"The worst part of this funeral is you,"* he said, little flecks of spit landing on my face.

I wiped my cheek, startled, but unwilling to show Mr. Whitman that I was upset. "Okay, I'll be right downstairs if you should need—"

"I don't want you up here. You got that?" he said, his bottom lip quivering. I'd seen plenty of clients struggle with loss, but this was out of control.

I shut myself in my office for the rest of the service. *I guess everyone grieves differently*, I told myself, trying to shake the confrontation off. *But what a dick.*

Business continued to tank. It wasn't that people weren't dying; that's one of the perks of working in funerals—you never have to worry about a demand shortage. The problem with Crawford, though, was that it was by far the most expensive place to bid adieu to a loved one. With the economy in the tank, suddenly people who wouldn't have even asked how much a casket cost were haggling down the prices—and in a lot of cases, taking their business elsewhere. Crawford might have been the best, but it wasn't the only player in the game.

I wasn't the only staffer losing faith. Monica took to calling out sick at least once a week, and some of the part-timers had moved on to different funeral homes after getting fed up with Tony constantly canceling their shifts because business was so slow. Inventory, which I'd never gotten the impression was a big deal, suddenly became a numbers crunch—and my responsibility. "Where can we cut?" Tony said, dumping the list on my desk now that I'd been unofficially demoted and was barely working with clients. "Find more ways to cut." Then he walked away, leaving me to figure out which would be worse to lose: tissues or toilet paper. A year earlier, orders had included sewing kits, tissue packets, and tiny bottles of hand sanitizer, all with customized Crawford labels, but now we were back to basics. *This is what my job has become*, I thought, growing increasingly bored . . . and uninspired.

"I can't do this anymore," I said to my mom over lunch. We met at a small French café around the corner from Crawford, since it didn't matter anymore if I skipped out for a couple of hours. Nobody even noticed.

"I'm not going to tell you to quit," she said, sipping her cappuccino. "But trust me, Elizabeth, it never hurts to consider more than one option in your life. You've proven yourself here. You can move on."

I had been holding on so tightly to this idea that I had to prove everyone wrong, to show them that my job at Crawford was really important and not just a phase. But now that I *had* done it, what was I clinging to? What was I trying to prove?

"I've been thinking about leaving New York," I said. In reality, the thought had vaguely passed my mind, usually when I was walking home in a stupor after a long, frustrating shift. This was the first time I had said it out loud. I braced myself for Mom's reaction.

"I think that would be great for you," she said.

I was so shocked, I dropped my fork. *Is she really supporting me in this?* I thought. I had expected her to say that was crazy, that I needed to get serious about my life. But here she was telling me to go. Knowing that my mom finally trusted me to make the right decisions in my life gave me a boost of confidence, and in a flash, what had seemed like an insane notion became a sorta-kinda amazing option.

A few days later, I was in my office, looking at a map of Europe on my computer. *Where could I go?* I thought, scanning the familiar cities. *What will I do?* I was in the middle of imagining myself planning grand funerals in Paris when one of the receptionists called in to say that we had a family coming in that afternoon to plan a service for their daughter, who had been a young trader on Wall Street. "They found her body in a flower bed," said the receptionist, sounding like she might cry. I was so used to death by that point that I thought, *Oh, kind of nice that she lay down in a pile of flowers in her last moment. Kind of poetic.*

Then I found out how she got in the flower bed: she jumped. From a seventeenth-floor balcony.

There had actually been a cluster of suicides, all on the same day. Apparently, a bunch of stocks were sent plummeting after a technical glitch occurred. It was corrected shortly after—maybe even just a matter of hours, if not minutes—but the error was enough to make some traders think that they had lost big money for their clients. If there were ever one thing that proved just how strung out New Yorkers had become, it was the fact that people were *killing themselves* over *other people's money*. They weren't living on the edge—they were working on the edge. And one gust could push them over.

We had another suicide call that same week. This time, it

was a lawyer at a big-time firm. He killed himself by sucking on a bunch of helium balloons and sticking his head in a bag. The family—like most families in cases of suicide—was a mix of sad, shocked, and protective. Their son had done everything right: summa cum laude undergrad, Harvard Law, got hired as an associate at one of the most famous law firms in the country. This was supposed to be when they could finally relax. They had laid a good egg, and he had hatched into the type of upstanding guy that his Jewish mom could set up with any socialite from the synagogue. Now he was dead, and they were left trying to figure out how to keep his cause of death under wraps.

The service was quiet and family only. They didn't invite any of the other associates or the partners from the firm, even though just about everyone in the field had heard *something* about what happened—whether it was the real version of events or not. Not that it mattered. Everyone was so busy hanging on to their jobs for dear life that they probably wouldn't have left the office to go to the service anyway. I saw this with Max firsthand—he wasn't just glued to his desk, he was cemented to the thing. Max had always been the one who was close to Mom, but now that she and I were on the same page again, Max was the one we were left worrying about. "How is he?" I'd ask.

She'd just shrug. "I'm starting to think they have him chained up over there."

Too many people around me weren't living any more

than the bodies I saw every day in caskets. One of the worst examples was Paul Wagner, a Wall Street guy who had preplanned his funeral back when people were shelling out the big bucks. He bought one of the $90,000 caskets, had expensive flowers ordered—the works. When he actually bit the bullet—not literally, in this case—we braced ourselves for a flood of friends and family. Surely a man with that kind of bank was well connected and would have people flocking to say good-bye. At least that's what I thought. The only person who showed up was his assistant. One person. The guy, who looked to be in his fifties, came in and signed the guest book and then said a private good-bye to the man who had employed him for the past twenty years. It was a small gesture with a major payoff: Paul had written in his will that his eight-figure estate was to be divided equally between anyone who signed the guest book at his funeral.

Still, there was something deeply sad, not about death, but about seeing someone die so alone. My dad's funeral had been so packed, people clogged not just the viewing room but the hallway *and* the foyer. There was so much love surrounding him that it was obvious his was a life well lived. What could be worse than dying and barely anyone caring? None of Paul's clients bothered to come, and he had made them millions. Making people rich doesn't make them your friends.

As I became more and more disillusioned with Crawford—and more and more aware that a shitty job can literally suck the life out of you—I thought about what leaving Crawford would mean. I saw so many problems with the funeral business, but at Crawford, it had become impossible to fix them. It was clear that I had come to the end of the line, and after thinking about my options, I finally had the perfect plan: business school . . . in London. I had been there over a dozen times, I loved the city, and . . . well . . . I spoke English. (Plus let's all just agree that a British accent is pretty damn sexy on a man.)

"I think business school is a fabulous plan," said Mom. She, Gaby, and I were having dinner at her place, noshing on stuffed salmon and fennel.

"Yes, and you need to clear your energy of Crawford," said Gaby, in the very Zen way she talks, like a yoga instructor. "Besides, I needed a better excuse than another party to fly out to London. Now I have one!"

"You aren't upset about me moving away?" I asked.

"Upset? The opposite," said Mom. "If you go to business school, I'll even pay for it. It's about time you got out of this city and . . . you know . . . *lived* a little. Maybe you'll even find a new passion."

I gave Mom a look and laughed. I was sure a small part of her—okay, fine, maybe a big part—was still hoping that I would change directions and go into consulting or some other career, but it wasn't happening. I loved the death business; helping families plan amazing funerals was my calling, and I wasn't about to give it up. What I really wanted to do was take some of the fear out of death for people and learn to run a business that didn't rely on hustling clients in a vulnerable time, but rather making that time *easier*. I had learned a lot at Crawford—that was for sure. But I also had the feeling that there just had to be a better way to do death.

Elaine was ecstatic to hear the news. "Oh thank God," she said on the phone from her condo in Palm Beach. I pictured her out on her balcony, wearing high-waist pants and a top with her ridiculous owl brooch pinned to it. "And *London*. I *love* London. You must *mustmustmust* go to Alain Ducasse—oh, the food is just marvelous. I would come out there to visit but you know, I have the Smirnoffs, and it just gets so dreary there in certain seasons . . ." I wasn't quite sure why I had called her in the first place; it just felt like I was making a big change in my life, and she should know. As a result, I had to listen to forty-five minutes of gossip about every old biddy in her bridge group.

Envisioning what my life would be like in London wasn't just exciting, it was easy: I already had wonderful friends there. I would hop the pond, rent a flat, and busy myself with business school classes. Ever since my dad had gotten sick, I had clung on to New York; it was the place where I felt most connected to him, and it was also my home, the place I felt most secure. But the more I thought about it, I realized that just about the last thing my adventurous father would have wanted was for me to take the safe route and stay put. If he were there, he would have said, "Why are you even thinking about it? Go!" And now with my family and friends behind me, there was only one thing left to do: quit Crawford.

I woke up feeling sick. Not, like, flu sick, or I-drank-three-too-many-vodkas sick, but just a nervous, terrible pit in my stomach. I didn't agree with everything Tony did in business, but he had been a mentor to me . . . and I was about to let him down. I rehearsed what I would say in the shower and while I blow-dried my hair. Then I opened my closet and laughed. Maybe it was because we sometimes don't see ourselves changing until the transformation has taken place, but it struck me just how far I'd come since my first day at Crawford; all of the furs and designer gowns were smushed together on the side, barely even reachable. Even my boxes of Jimmy Choos and Manolos were pushed away to make room for a line of ugly black Aerosoles flats. This had become my normal, and even though Crawford had been tough, it had also been worth it. I'd become a person I never even knew I had in me: strong, good under pressure, even more compassionate.

I put on my blazer and made the five-minute walk to Crawford. *You've got this*, I told myself, still a bit nervous but knowing for sure that I was doing the right thing. But before I talked to Tony, I wanted to let Bill know that I was leaving. I found him in the prep room (of course), already turning a stroke victim into a rosy-cheeked beauty.

"Bill," I sighed, leaning in the doorway. I knew that I would miss him the most—especially the moments of the two of us dancing around the prep tables, gossiping and strategizing the Giants' trade options.

"Lizzie, why so glum?" he said, bobbing his head to the music.

"I'm not glum," I said.

He looked up from the body. "You look pretty glum. More drama upstairs? Tell Monica that she can take an empanada and shove it up her—"

"No, no, no," I laughed. "Bill, I'm about to quit."

He rested the tube pumping the embalming fluid on the table and put his hands on his hips.

"Well, I'll be damned," he said. "You finally did it. I'm proud of you, kid."

"Proud of me? But I'm quitting," I said. I wanted to tell him how much his friendship had meant to me, but I couldn't bring myself to get all sappy. Instead I just told him that I was going to go to London to "study some business." "I'll miss seeing you all the time," I finally said.

Bill smiled and held his arms out to give me a hug. "Well, we'll always have Paris."

I laughed. "I'm not going to Paris, I'm going to *London*," I said. "And you better not come near me with those gloves covered in God knows what."

We both laughed. It was a drama-free good-bye, just like it had been a drama-free friendship. I don't know that I would have made it through my time at Crawford without Bill keeping me sane.

I walked out of the prep room and down the hall, taking everything in. The air still smelled like lilies and carpet cleaner, just like it had when I'd walked in to plan Dad's funeral, but *I* was different now. Asking for a job at Crawford had been something I'd done on a whim when I was desperate to find myself. But I was no longer searching. Whether I liked it or not, it was within Crawford's walls that I'd figured out how to move on with a life that no longer included my dad. In the years after his death, this was the place where I became myself again . . . just a better, weirder version.

The sentimental feeling was replaced by an overall queasiness as I approached Tony's office. We hadn't been speaking much—the guy had been flat-out avoiding me—and suddenly there I was, about to tell him that I was leaving. I'd never had to quit a job before; I didn't know what to say, just what I *thought* I should say.

"I have to talk to you," I said, taking a deep breath. *It's a job. People quit jobs. It's not personal*, I thought, giving myself a mental pep talk.

"This isn't really a great time. We've got a service this afternoon I've got to get ready for," said Tony.

I stopped straight in front of his desk. I had prepared it all so perfectly, word for word. I would be calm and straightforward and professional. I would be unemotional but kind and grateful. Instead, I opened my mouth, and all that came out was, "How do I give my two weeks' notice?"

Tony looked at me in silence for a good ten seconds. "I think you just did," he said.

I braced myself for what I was sure would come next—an onslaught of "how could you's" and "after all we've done for you's"—but instead Tony just stood up, looked me in the eyes, and held out his hand. "I've never worked with someone like you," he said. "We're going to miss you around here."

Rather than shake his hand, I held my arms out for a hug. Soon, we were both laughing. "I think we both know *everyone* here is not going to miss me."

"So what's next?" he asked, sitting back down.

"I'm thinking business school," I said. "Shake things up a little."

Tony smiled. "That is what you do best."

MY PLANE for London was leaving in three hours, and Mom was still running around the apartment, double-checking that I had outlet converters and enough La Mer body lotion to butter up an elephant (as if they don't have dry skin in England). I had already shipped boxes of my clothes—there was no way I could fit them all in a couple of suitcases—so all I had was one large bag, and then a tote for a carry-on. I packed the latter with my engraved Moleskine notebooks, my wallet, and my favorite photo. It was a picture of my mom, my dad, Max, Maggie, and me at the country house. We were sitting on the porch with the wind whipping our hair around, tan and smiling and *happy*. The photo reminded me that you never know when a good thing in your life is going to end; all you can do is enjoy the moment and appreciate what you have right there, right then.

"Are you sure you're going to be okay?" I asked Mom, who was now folding the cashmere shawl she always wore around the house.

"Elizabeth, I miss your father every day," she said. "But he loved me enough for a lifetime. It was enough. It *is* enough. Don't worry about me." She held out the loved garment and motioned for me to take it.

"But that's your favorite," I said.

"It's freezing in London," she said. "Do your 'mum' a favor and take the shawl so I don't have to worry about you huddled by some nineteenth-century heater."

I unfolded the shawl and wrapped it around me.

"The mostest," she said.

My eyes welled with tears. That had been what my father used to say when I dressed up for formal events. It started when I was eight years old. I'd walked down the hall wearing a blue dress with a wide sash and asked my father, "Do I look beautiful?" After that, every time we went somewhere fancy together, we played out the same routine. By the time I was in high school, I didn't even have to ask—he would just see me dressed up and say, "The mostest."

The car was waiting for me outside. I kissed and petted Maggie one last time; checked again that I had my phone, wallet, and passport; and wrapped the shawl more tightly around me. "I love you so much, I'll call you when I land," I said to my mom before handing my bag to the elevator man and riding it down to the lobby with him. "Here's to another adventure," I said to my dad, looking up. It was hard to believe it'd only been a few months since I'd left Crawford. It hadn't left me. I received at least one call or e-mail a week about so-and-so's parent or grandparent who had passed away. People wanted my help, and I loved being the person they could rely on to make a memorable send-off possible. Maybe I really was a little weird and a little morbid. Whatever the case, I knew that the funeral business was where I was meant to be, and I couldn't wait to give it a major makeover. No more ugly floral arrangements or money-grubbing men in suits. No more boring, formulaic eulogies or weepy music that makes you want to throw back a few Xanax. Death could be a heartbreaking, overpriced sob fest . . . or it could be a celebration.

I, for one, was ready for a good party.

Postmortem

*U*ntil someone close to you dies, it's impossible to know what that loss will feel like—and so the thought of death is terrifying, at least for most people. I can see now, four years since I left Crawford, that taking a job at a funeral home was my way of not clinging to but rather moving on from my dad's death. I needed to know death. I needed to understand it. I needed to stop fearing it, and my way of doing that was to help other people who were grieving.

You know how there are those relationships where the couple likes to stay in, watching movies and ordering takeout, just calm and steady? And then there are other couples who are either all over each other or in a heated argument? The latter is my relationship with Crawford. Now that we're broken up, so to speak, I have to remind myself of the bad moments—the Monica drama, the crazy hours, my alleged affair with Tony—because it's so easy to remember all of the good. Even now, when I enter a funeral home, I still have the urge to fix the flowers and critique the makeup job on the body (in all seriousness, *no one* is as good as Bill). I also never leave the house without a Kleenex in my purse, in case someone near me starts crying. It's a grief reflex I can't—and don't want to—turn off.

After Crawford, I did exactly what I set out to do: I spent a year in London, got my MBA, and started plotting how to plan funerals *my* way. And I got some practice earlier than I anticipated. Elaine called me in London, saying, "Lizzie, I'm dying. And considering everyone else in our world seems to think you're the best at dealing with this, one would at least assume you would handle your own grandmother's funeral."

Elaine had a flair for the dramatic up until the very end, so I had to ask: "Dying right now? Or dying like we're all dying? You know I'm across the Atlantic, right?"

"Lovey girl, you know what I mean," she said, her voice sounding even deeper and raspier than usual. The woman had smoked at least a pack of Benson & Hedges cigarettes (the ones that come in a gold box—of course) every day for the past sixty years. All those puffs had caught up with her.

I'd forgiven Elaine for bailing on Dad in his last moments as much as I could, but I'd never forgotten it. "Nanny, look. I'm meant to come home from London in two weeks,"

I said. "If it's an emergency, I will get on a plane now. If it's not, I will see you in two weeks."

Elaine sighed loudly. "Fiiine. I'll wait."

I flew straight from Heathrow to Palm Beach, where I found Elaine in a silk nightgown, her hair still perfectly done up, wearing coral-pink lipstick that matched her flawlessly manicured nails. She must have made the nurse double as a beautician, because there was no way she had done them herself. By this point, Elaine was mostly bedridden—although you'd never know it from her attitude. She acted more like a woman of leisure napping away the afternoon than a sick person. To be fair, she was keeping with her style.

As I spent a few days in Palm Beach, Elaine's condition worsened. I called Max and told him to book a flight down. "If you want to say good-bye, I think you should come now," I told him. Max had a similar relationship with Elaine as I did—he loved her, mostly out of obligation, but had never felt that warm, fuzzy feeling a grandma is supposed to give her grandkids. This was, after all, the woman who, when we'd visited as kids, would have "the help" set out a crudité platter and chopped liver, as if two children under the age of twelve wanted to munch on snap peas and oniony organs. Chocolate chip cookies? Not a chance. She probably thought Toll House was a private party venue.

Elaine was very clear on her preferences. She wanted to die in Palm Beach and then be shipped up to Crawford's sister funeral home in New York, which was more popular with Jewish families. She specifically wanted a graveside service. Only me, Max, and close family should speak. "Did you write that down, lovey girl?" she said. "I don't want just anyone up there blabbing away, blah, blah, blah."

As she deteriorated, I called hospice. They upped her morphine. It could have been that I'd gotten weirdly too comfortable with death, or maybe it was just that Elaine wasn't Grandmother of the Year, but her last days weren't a particularly emotional time. I made sure she wasn't in pain and that the nurses were doing their jobs. She made sure to occasionally open her eyes and say something, just to remind me she wasn't dead yet. When her breathing finally slowed, I prepared for a heartfelt good-bye. Instead, Elaine opened one eye, looked up at Max and me, and gave a half-smile. "Shalom!" she said. And then she was gone.

FOR THE MOST PART, my two lives—one in the funeral business, the other at society parties—rarely collide outside of Crawford. People just don't like to talk about death at social functions; it makes the champagne taste bad. But one recent exception to this rule was the night my friend was hosting an event at his newly opened restaurant. It was a big scene—the sort of event that draws celebrities, writers, artists, investors, CEOs . . . the works. And while my friend was one of the hosts, he didn't have a date. "I will look like a loser if I go to this alone," he said. "And I can't bring some rando." Even though I'd grown to dread stuffy events (how many times do I need to stand in a circle with a bunch of women I barely know telling each other, "That juice cleanse is really working for you! And that dress! Mmm. *Superb*"), I wanted to support him, so I agreed to be his date.

I'd been seated next to an important guest my friend was trying to impress. (Nobody sits next to her date at these things anyway; it's considered antisocial.) She was a socialite, but also a writer for a prestigious magazine. And my friend, well, he wanted what any venue owner in this city wants—a glowing review from someone who matters.

I recognized her before I sat down, and my heart dropped. Would she remember me? The woman—I'll call her Victoria—gave me the once-over and then, sipping her glass of white wine, said, "So, do you work? Or do you just do *this*?" She stuck her pointer finger out from her grasp on the wineglass, looking disdainfully around the room. I felt proud that I wasn't just a girl who partied for a living, like some of my friends, and took a deep breath. "Actually, I work in the funeral business. You know, Crawford Funeral Home?" I said, watching her reaction closely.

Victoria looked at me again, this time taking in my face instead of my dress. Her eyes filled with tears and her lip quivered.

"I know," I said, gently putting my hand on her back. "How are you and your daughter doing?"

A year and a half earlier, I had helped Victoria plan a

close family member's funeral. As soon as the connection was clear, her tears turned into a full cry, so I asked her if she'd like me to take her to the restroom. (There was always plenty of drama at society events, but one rule always applied: never be the woman crying at the table.) After she finally calmed down and blotted her eyes with the tissue I'd handed her from my purse, Victoria turned to me. "You need to explain yourself," she said. "I would think a Crawford employee would need to sneak into a party like this."

I told her my story—the short version, anyway—standing against the sinks in the ladies' room. A few weeks later, she wrote a piece about me for the magazine. Some people read it and dismissed me. I get it. It's easy to take a quick look and write me off as another mindless rich girl getting her hands dirty for attention, and that's exactly what some readers did. They made fun of my Gucci shoes and called me silly and shallow. The negativity took some getting used to, but at the end of the day, life's too short. It's too short to get upset about what other people think . . . too short not to do what makes you happy . . . too short to not call that person back, to stay angry, to hold a grudge. And—I can say this now that my mom is one of my best friends—it's *definitely* too short to resent the only parent you have.

But the best part about my unexpected career in the death business is that my dad would have loved it! He always encouraged me to embrace my quirkiness—one of his favorite sayings was "When the world zigs, zag." If I could still pick up the phone and call him (the way I want to every single day; I can still recite his number by heart), I know he would say he's proud of me.

Now I advise private clients and consult tech companies in the end-of-life industry. My biggest goal? To make death less scary by changing the business itself. I always say the topic of death is like that of sex was in the 1950s; nobody talked about it, but everyone was doing it.

I've spoken at universities, written columns, even chatted about funerals on the radio. My absolute favorite part of what I do is acting as a liaison between grieving families and funeral directors; I feel like I'm one of the few people who can truly understand both sides, and I like to think I help make a heavy process a little less weighty. This might be a weird job, but screw it . . . I'm a weirdo. I'd much rather be a contrarian than the person I could have become—another girl, with another cocktail, acting like lunching on the Upper East Side is a career. Instead, I've found my strange, wonderful calling. And even though death might not be the way *most* people make a living, I would just about die doing anything else.

Acknowledgments

The biggest thank-you goes to my family. My late father, Brett, whose passing inspired me to enter the funeral industry, would have loved and supported my career more than anyone. My work is a testament to my never-ending love for him. The numerous values he instilled continue to guide me, and I hope he rests in peace. My mom, Patricia, has stayed with me on this roller coaster; always there to celebrate the ups and support me through the downs. She became my strongest advocate, not only sending me every death-related article (and trekking to countless funeral homes) but also doing it with a smile. I could never thank her enough for usually appreciating but always loving me. *Good Mourning* would not exist without my brother, Damon, who trusted me to follow my heart. Without his unwavering support, I would not have found a career that I am so passionate about, or mustered up the self-esteem to advocate for myself. His witty naming of this book and his comments were most appreciated. Working in death makes you appreciate the importance of family during life. I would like to express my gratitude to my extended family on both my mother's and father's sides. You have all influenced me deeply, and any attempt to mention each of you by name would certainly result in me overlooking someone.

When it came to actually putting *Good Mourning* on paper, I was fortunate enough to get exquisite editorial craftsmanship and guidance from my skillful and generous inner team, Cait, Cait, and Kate. Caitlin Moscatello's ("Writer Cait") incredible skills are just part of what she brought to this project. She's a gifted writer and now a dear friend, and I thank her for laughing and crying with me as she dedicated countless hours to unraveling and retelling my story. Thanks to everyone at Creative Artists Agency who helped to turn my story into a book. I couldn't have done this without Cait Hoyt ("Agent Cait"), who passionately guided a first-time author and championed this project. I'd also like to thank Phil Cohen for all his help and Tiffany Ward, Vanessa Silverton-Peel, Michelle Kroes, and Brittany Patch for their ongoing enthusiasm. *Good Mourning* would still just be an idea and not an actual book if it weren't for the support of Jen Bergstrom and the talented team at Simon & Schuster, especially Kate Dresser ("Editor Kate"), whose keen insights and edits were always welcome and extremely helpful.

Dad regularly reiterated the phrase "No matter what, call the lawyer," so a heartfelt thank you goes to David Fritz ("Lawyer David") for constantly guiding and supporting me. By handling all my questions and issues with a casual positivity characteristic of my dad's, he filled a void and empowered me to move forward. The assistance he and his business partner, Jason Boyarski, offer is truly phenomenal.

Many thanks to my friends Ameesha, Amunjeet, Cristina, Flavia, Jen, Pam, and Priyanka for appreciating the towering flower arrangements, accepting my black suits, listening to my bizarre stories, and then pushing me to retell them to the world. A "good old-fashioned" thank you to Chris Barish. Josh Adam, thank you for constantly reminding me: "We never had to take any of it seriously."

My father's sense of humor and lust for life lives on in Mark Locks ("Uncle Tiger"). I am forever grateful to him for keeping me by his side (at some particularly fabulous events) and watching over me—I could not appreciate it more.

My life would be a mess without the vital global guidance, support, and assistance of Professor Joseph Lampel and Jas Kaur in London, Jason Latos and Patty Merritt at UBS in Manhattan, Nikola Barisic and Jeb Brien in Los Angeles, and Clayton Chaffee in the Berkshires. Thank you to Saima Meyer for the love she has brought to my family. I so appreciate the lifetime of support and laughter that Gabriele

Gidion has given me. I would also very much like to thank the entire team at Everplans.com, especially Adam Seifer, Abby Schneiderman, Gene Newman, Mike, Warren, and Ammon for providing me with the time and encouragement that was necessary for me to complete this endeavor.

I entered the funeral industry knowing nothing about it. I am forever grateful to those who believed that a naïve yet passionately empathic young girl was worthy of their time and training. I would particularly like to thank Steve, Mr. Charles, Dominic, Rob, and Catherine for their incomparable guidance. Finally, thank you to all in this field who guided me, and who, more importantly, assist families in their most difficult times each and every day.

Elizabeth Meyer

After working at an elite funeral home in New York City, Elizabeth became passionate about making death a less taboo topic, and is now a licensed funeral director. She regularly contributes to news articles, speaks on national syndicated radio programs, and has given guest lectures about death and dying. Currently, she advises private clients and consults for a website that deals with end-of-life issues. Elizabeth holds a BA from New York University's Gallatin School, an MBA from Cass Business School in London, and a certification in thanatology from the Association for Death Education and Counseling. She was raised and currently resides in Manhattan.

Caitlin Moscatello

Caitlin Moscatello is a writer and editor whose work has appeared in *Glamour*; *Marie Claire*; *O, The Oprah Magazine*; *Self*; *Redbook*; *Sports Illustrated*; and other publications. She lives in Manhattan.